Smile!

More than Something!

to Peter
& all that is good
about architectural
education

An environmentally friendly book printed and bound in England by
www.printondemand-worldwide.com

This book is made entirely of chain-of-custody materials

www.fast-print.net/store.php

SMILE! THE NEW PHILOSOPHY
Copyright © Dr Bill Thompson 2014

Cover illustration by Georgina Trevor

All characters are fictional.
Any similarity to any actual person is purely coincidental.

The right of Dr Bill Thompson to be identified as the author of this work has
been asserted by him in accordance with the Copyright, Designs and
Patents Act 1988 and any subsequent amendments thereto.

A catalogue record for this book is available from the British Library

ISBN 978-178456-119-2

First published 2014 by
FASTPRINT PUBLISHING
Peterborough, England.

Smile!

More than Something!

by

Dr. Bill Thompson

Contents

Illustrations

Prologue

Way Beyond Semiotics

After a shortish holiday in the south of France the book that I took with me to revise a little has been completely re-written or is in train of being so.

This was agonizing, but useful since part of the plan was to catch up on reading several books, amongst them one by Zizek, "less than nothing".

Conversations with close friends, in English I have to say, further provoked the feeling I had that the script I took with me was not good enough. It has been scrapped as text but not as my personal experience of what it took to arrive at that point when I left London some days ago.

So this is the result of not only ten years of study as a student with students of *my* cultural context course in Belfast school of architecture at Ulster university <u>and</u> four years of research at home and in the British library which is close by home, and finally a sort of gestation or even a birth in the south of France 2014.

The title of the work generally has been Smile for a while now, but the subtitle of the first of three, *"more than something"*, is partly a response to Zizek's title *"less than nothing"*, which will become more obvious as the trilogy, of which this is the first volume, develops between now and 2015, the topic being the architecture of socialisation.

Wednesday, 24 September 2014

The Introduction
The Gist of the Chapters

Salut, Zizek[1] and Einstein! Their contributions need to be taken further. Time and space is something we create ourselves. There is just movement, so if and when it stops there is nothing. Contingency is the starting point of all movement since an understanding of nothing could turn out to be anything in the midst of everything moving.

The relative condition between movements of various kinds emerges from the contingent possibility that all movement distinguishes moving differently. We are each aware of movement, and become equally aware that we learn to appreciate movement and that some are limited whilst others seem not, and all in context; thus **more than something** as the subtitle to this the first volume of a trilogy of books. This first is a rough and ready description of the neural system articulated by an architect who found none of the existing rational and instrumental explanations acceptable, even after reading many other disciplinary contributions, as architects often do, a few of which appear in the appendix to each volume with gratitude. I always thought there must be **something more** and **something else**, and of course these will be the sub titles of my other books in the trilogy!

---

[1] I have to say that I am still just half way through "less than nothing", so I cannot say that my position on this won't change, however I can't see how at this point, having read some other works of his choosing and now half of this one but we shall see, as we do.

In Chapter one I explain **<u>sui-generis.</u>** I understand this as the relationship in which contingency is what is happening. We experience living. It is happening to us and we wish to know what it is but it always requires a context, because all movement emerges from sui-generis and is thus unknowable until it happens, and no use unless it repeats itself. What we refer to as phenomena is the effect of removing contingency at certain scales of relativity so that they become fixed for us. We process our appreciation of movements, and they become known as relative categories because we need to regularise what is happening if we can so that we can cope with living. We are the products of regular movements in myriad causal chains intersecting, interrupting, and all those other words we seem able to use and share in order to articulate a sort of milieu within which phenomena emerge so that we call ourselves, or are called, functional or hopelessly dysfunctional, apprentices to functionality by hand and brain, labourers, workers. **<u>Sui-generis</u>** is the constant that is the immediate present and movement is happening. Thus any thing fixed is a chimera produced out of nothing but movement.

Chapter two explains **<u>symbiosis</u>** as the process whereby we accommodate appearances that emerge out of sui-generis and have appeared to us as a result of our contextual relationship to those appearances. The relevance of contexts become apparent to each of us as the maker of values linked to the appearances we experience. I use **<u>symbiosis</u>** to share the concept of the accumulation of the values of what appears to us and the storage of its appearance individually. In the next part of the process, synergy, we convert accumulated mass experience into phenomena, harvesting experience accumulated as a personal resource. These phenomena are produced in the same way by all of us by a remarkable similarity of processing in each of us since each one of us is a repeat performance of what has been repeated for around sixty thousand years[2] specifically, and generally as upright walkers for four million years. The actual conversion of appearances into phenomena must remain individual hence there are some almost pathological instances of what that processing produces as phenomena yet we must avoid the term, pathological, if we are **all** to be considered human, since that is important for the human condition, it must be inclusive of us all. What we appear to have in common is the accumulation of experience as a part/context value of all those appearances and these are shunted around our bodies individually, uniquely, as chemical and electrical changes creating quantitative change in mass value [the construct] with categorical fragmentation into departments so as to provide a resource for the subject of the next chapter, synergy, as I understand the process[3].

In Chapter three I explain **synergy** as the further processing that takes the departmentalised mass value, using hand and brain according to complex systems, creating phenomena that become dialectically reflexive to what is happening as a result of this combination of synergy and symbiosis [process]. This is

---

[2] I use Bickerton for this figure of 60,000 – [see list of books]

[3] As always in this spectacular subject we will not know exactly how we manage to use and share or even create phenomena until much more forensic work is done and even at that time, as now, extrapolation [sensible guessing] will play a large part in any shared understanding, so this is really just a preview of what I believe will be discovered and/or what has already been discovered and reported in the contributions of others!

the effect of what synergy does to what symbiosis did and did before, so that appearances and values relate to phenomena that we have produced for ourselves in contexts that alter. These phenomena, that are already part of a now continuous processing by each individual, in turn being a repeat of all similar processing by all similar repeat beings, humans, become the "phenomena" that we are aware of as part context and potentially part whole[4]. We all create phenomena out of the appearances that relative movements bring to symbiosis and synergy returns to symbiosis creating a dialectical process unique to each of us and yet common to our race, appearances processed into phenomena out of the dialectic between experience and construct [ongoing mass experience] and sui-generis [nothing] and context[5].

I am not sure at the moment how our extrapolation of the processing carried out by symbiosis and synergy together, as a circular process forever experienced between sui-generis and construct, evolved until it was able to produce such a complex extrapolated articulation as we now contrive to live by, although all animals do this. I do give a few suggestions based on the contributions already made by others when I refer to its effect as **incorporation** in chapter four. I suggest that incorporation is the extended activity of the dialectic[6], dealing with what I call limited and unlimited part/pattern relationships that can be nested, patterns becoming parts of greater patterns, and categorised according to the two forms of action, work and labour, thus having scales of both category

---

[4] Though note that the only universal infinite truth is nothing, sui-generis
[5] This is prior to what Badiou uses for his "material dialectic"
[6] Whereas this is possibly Badiou's "material dialectic"

and context such that labouring by hand and brain has such a huge influence on overall outcomes especially in the area of political economic wisdom[7] by refusing the limitations of work, functionality. In fact we could say that political economic wisdom is only possible at any meaningful global scale for humanity as a whole, if we can link the two categories of work and labouring together so that we never totalise functionality, never make part/context into part/whole. Whereas this greater complexity is accounted for by our ability to create programmes using qualitative phenomena categorically and quantitatively contextually in global articulations that effectively restrict our freedom to explore-and-make-mistakes. The dialectical process out of which all phenomena emerge provides us with existential challenges, i.e. for us to work, to function we have to become reflexive, and remain free only by acknowledging understanding is ambiguous and not a systemic whole.

In Chapter five, I discuss the consequences of using and sharing extrapolations as a **solidarity** which is the socialisation that individuals become part of using a political economic wisdom and not simply wisdom for and/or of the individual. For example the individual may feel that their own reflexive limited life is the only possible way of living. This is explored in Chapter six, which is the struggle an individual experiences when attempting to deal with the extrapolation reflexively in the context of incorporation challenged by incommensurate solidarities. The struggle to alter the reflexive

---

[7] This is that we are capable of effecting the results of any creative action upon the world in which we live with affective outcomes.

dialectic, using a process that requires limitation yet has access to unlimited appearances, leads to complex and often contradictory and paradoxical performances that all too easily become overly rational and instrumental, typically and erroneously relating to one extrapolation transcendentally overcoming the dialectic. In short socialisation becomes reflexivity because the aim of incorporation becomes making extrapolation whole, reflexive for functionality, so that all labouring is converted into work. The aim of solidarity is to refer to taking advantage of the dialectic/reflexive for a group. Hence in order to incorporate, individuals must cease incorporating other than socially, shall we say, and use the dialectic to maintain an extrapolation that both science and philosophy acknowledge cannot be licensed as whole. The point about individual wisdom then, is that it must be aware of solidarity and even incorporation because in order to achieve functionality the individual must become a machine whereas the individual is a process. At this point of course it is possible that the individual is also individually wise and thus able to join incorporations and solidarities and yet keep their extrapolations contingent, knowing they are never whole, understanding the consequences and responsibilities of becoming functional in either case, which is ineluctably a necessary or desirable part of the extrapolation in order to justify the claim to wisdom [which means that the individual could be dialectically transcendental to the essential repetition involved in work, incorporation and solidarity, reflexive and yet creative, a mastery of the human dialectic[8]].

---

[8] This is the condition known as "accomplished nihilism" I believe but would appear to be difficult to master in both limited and transcendental

In my final chapter seven, the architecture of socialisation, I explore the consequences of my belief that all extrapolations start with appearances, move through the human dialectical processing that is symbiosis and synergy, with appearances becoming phenomena, emerging as reflexive and/or apprenticed incorporation and solidarity in the material dialectic. This explains how behaviourist metrics[9] and psychiatric neural calisthenics[10] are possible whilst at the same time explaining how the location of any source of these remains a complete and utter mystery unless they are understood as outlined here.

The innate fungibility of the individual, thus the adaptive and improvisational nature of human processing that we have, means political economic wisdoms are always only a conversation with ourselves and other individuals or their commodification/quantification into what matters for rationalisation and instrumentalism to succeed implying that there must be a reduction of processing, a reduction in labouring and an increase in working, for rationalism and instrumentalism to succeed at all. We perform actions, of hand and brain on what is happening altering the human dialectic along with the material. Thus political economic wisdom relies upon understanding that individual wisdom is an ally or nemesis of wisdom and vice-versa, which most of us already know, of course, to our cost, or advantageously. It also means

---

categories.

[9] Measuring phenomena as if they are the basis of function, rather than the product of the human dialectic and thus open to processing.

[10] The in my view false belief that we can rationalise or instrumentalise as whole what we have just avowed is contingent and thus open.

that both forms of wisdom, limited and unlimited are contingent upon the labouring that gives work of any sort its meaning; that in effect we ourselves are most free when we are creative, not reflexive, and become less and less free the more we work rather than labour; i.e. we must delimit our human dialectical power rather than limit it, since we appear to have a propensity to limit the material dialectic once it is fully functional making all socialisations conversations between us for good and ill alike. Thus socialism, conservatism and pragmatism are one and the same effect of the human condition. Socialisation is what alters the material condition of humans by making functional what is possible and individuals take account of its consequences or they do not. Thus the control of value becomes seminal to any democratic materialism as well as to any despot.

Chapter One
Sui Generis

Humanities emergence came out of difference between us and the biological resource that was available previously, a genetic shift that altered the use of hand and brain. The boundary of what can be rational was altered for us, the boundary of instrumental was altered for us, and we responded using the same dialectical process as before except now it had different resources, phenomena that we made for ourselves, a human dialectic. Those resources require reflexivity to shift from coping with experience by labouring to coping by working functionally using hand and brain. There is a creative tension between extrapolation and the articulation of appearances and phenomena by hand and brain. Order requires dialectical reflexivity, creativity requires dialectical entropy, human and material. Creativity requires us to let go of order in favour of chaos, in a controlled way if we are to master the process and not simply mess up.

In 1865 concepts of entropy, and later statistical mechanics, emerged out of classical scientific belief[11], which until then had focussed on a mechanics believed to work because reflexive dialectical extrapolations can be disseminated and maintained using the media we create such as those used in reading and writing. The implication of what is in effect a model of experience or history succeeds mostly because it is readily open to accumulation and dialectical processing. The delusion it produces is that we exist within a time-line in universal space

---

[11] Mitchell M

and cope with this using something called a conscious mind if rational or a brain/body and some sort of programming or conditioning [education] if instrumental. The concept of simply being awake and asleep is ignored. Some philosophy put crudely perhaps, tends to focus upon the blood and soil metaphor as an integral part of a universal cosmology in which the whole is the race of human beings. This leads to some spirit of mind or body that links us to the soil by believing that programmes of work are made for us, typically referred to as instrumentalism or rationality. As we shall see in this text, the use of transcendentalism, work that is materially based, takes us away from the basic creativity used by our ancestors some 60,000 years before now so that to commence with rhetoric, to argue over what souls, spirits and beliefs **are** will miss the main point; which is that creativity related to limitation, delimitation and socialisation. It is no longer sufficient to ask what a phenomenon is, what is it? We must ask what is happening, are we exploring the human dialectic? This is a dynamic action of hand and brain linked to roots and growth with trial and error in the middle sandwiched between limitation and delimitation; pattern as context and pattern as whole being the dialectical process leading to materialism.

Sui generis requires the belief that all experience is the product of movement and existence is a chimera, a feeling of the real that can never truly be fixed as a whole except as nothing. This means that space and time are themselves merely but impressively, products of our ability to create phenomena out of movement by using part/pattern relationships since that is the only available resource available to processing. Moreover how do we repeat the creative process such that phenomena are re/created without massive contingency in that process? How do we resist what happens to change them repeatedly? These days, as against the days before Freud made his contribution to the human understanding, we are a lot more relaxed about what we call subliminal and aleatory appearances, those that push us towards labouring rather than work, rock the boat, upset the apple cart, force delimitation upon us. Since the 'us' in this is also movement based, the I and the me, that are also the experience of what is happening to me, we begin to appreciate a non-contingent part of movement that may even repeat in particular ways that indicates some regularity which we are able to master and cope with, the sun for example. Thus we can no longer say that absolutely all movement is contingent, we have to alter that understanding to say that the movement that we experience appears to be repetitive for three to five score years whereas other movement, such as dark and light, comes and goes repetitively on a daily basis and has limits of some sort. Our understanding of these regularities becomes an asset and perhaps an anxiety according to the experience we have of the consequences.

Rather than being an individual that perceives phenomena it seems we are without doubt processors that easily become reflexively inclined so we experience appearances as phenomena. This processing can become in the main reflexive, automatic, thus repetitive, potentially at least, set up genetically so that what I call symbiosis and synergy [see next chapters] operate a dialectic and we put down roots and harvest growth as a result. We can be comfortable in the knowledge that at least the body we have will keep repeating itself over and over again harvesting our reproductive abilities.

Individuals in pubs and at parties often seem pleased to comment on the quick replacement, repetitive growth, of some body parts such as the liver. We say, although from what I have read not totally accurately, the entire body is replaced over a seven year period[12]. It is true apparently that much of our body is in a constant state of replication based on DNA and the processes that relate to it. Whether we know about DNA or not seems to be irrelevant does it not? Of course, when we look at DNA and the associated phenomena we find that it and the associated phenomena owe their existence to pure movement that acts reflexively and contextually. The more we look for substance the more phenomena become thin air, or more accurately smaller and smaller phenomena, until we get to infinitely small phenomena which at the moment "we" are searching for in three countries using an accelerator, the search for the higgs-boson particle, which will inevitably turn out to be more movement that we can only experience on specialised machines. Pure energy must look rather like nothing in order to produce everything.

Yes, there is a theory as to how we get something from nothing, it is listed in one of the books in the book list appended to the end of this one[13]. Part of its contribution is the acceptance of complexity theory which is another contribution, also listed in the appendix[14]. It says explicitly that if we try to

---

[12] The brain cells, neurons, for example are not although axons grow and die
[13] Krauss L M
[14] Mitchell M

map what happens we remove most of might have happened in order to create a clean enough account of it. Movement at zero, nothing, is the only unity and it is empty of happenings. In effect we experience various movements that emerge for us as myriad appearances that we process into phenomena. In other words the concept of a whole universe is not possible as a totality because each of the parts appearing to us have different beginnings and different ends. This is a radical change from statements such as in the beginning of the universe. There is no beginning or end since there is only movement that is both relative and repetitive or not. Epicentres emerge as movements appear as patterns with edges and a centre or centres that help create the illusion of a whole.

Understanding is we could say, contingent, and is better described as experience that we can transcend using media to create an understanding that we share articulating phenomena we make. We process phenomena into mechanical extrapolations that **transcend** contingency in that we remove most of what might happen in order to create a clean, ordered, programme of action. Even our own lives bear testimony to this, the fact that we grow old means that our replication can be assessed and explained as a whole series of interactive part/pattern movements, heart, lungs, musculature, brain, body, that keeps us alive as individuals and yet age us in the same process and eventually kill us with eulogies. The paradox of Schrödinger's cat in the box of death is our conversion of experience into an answer rather than accepting paradox.

For the purpose of changing the way we think about living we have to move away from believing that we are and believe that we are a dialectical process between experience and sui-generis. We must believe that everything we believe has contingency about it that we limit in order to have order. We have to start producing a different sort of understanding. For example light passes through a window but we smash the glass. Why doesn't the light smash the glass when it passes through it? This is an understanding in which light and bodies move differently. It is 299,792,458m/sec compared to 125m/sec, see in diagram 1.1 below -

Diagram 1.1 Relative speeds within the nervous system

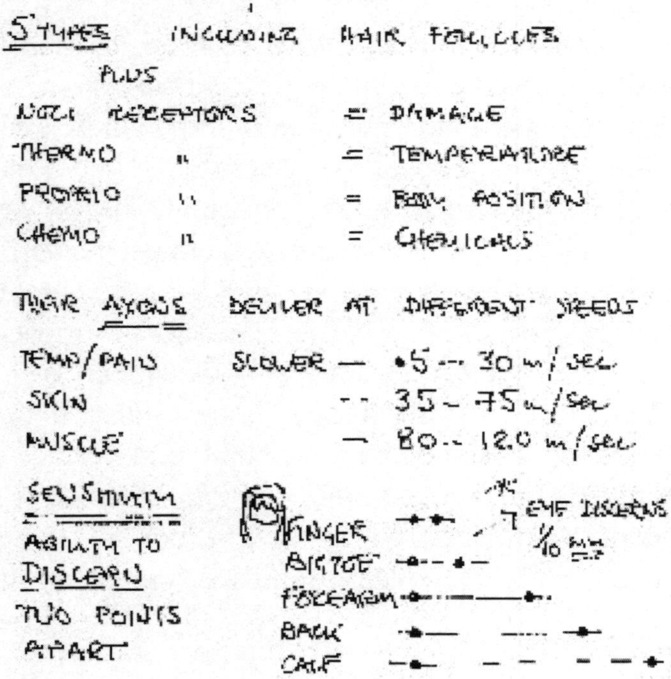

I grant you a universe unified as truth in nothing is a difficult concept to grasp mainly because we are constantly expected to believe that we are observing something because we keep transcending experience by limiting it. We come to believe we are observing what appears to us rather than that it is the dialectical processing of our asset, harvested experience, and synergy transcending that asset combining it with symbiosis, current experience and cleaning it up to make order out of any milieu. Understanding this sort of complexity is useful in order to show that complexity theory has a point, what happens depends upon the cleaning process. Hence time and space are the result of us cleaning up what appears to us as chaotic. As a result of our processing we are sometimes able to clarify appearances by dialectic interaction into specific part/whole relationships.

There is never any understanding other than the contingent, or if you prefer existence is the result of movement and so it is experience [of movement] and what we understand of it depends upon the processing that creates phenomena for us which we will call transcendental[15]. If we can grasp values in that process, which we do in the dialectical processing, then the body can do what Maxwell's demon is supposed to do and make phenomena move intelligently on their own so that they arrive at different parts of the same body as if guided by an invisible hand, the demon itself, the delusion that such a demon is necessary for the outcome. We know that we tag

[15] This was the contribution made by both Hegel and Kant following the big narcissism of the post blood and soil workers after say, the 15th century

experiences with both values and appearance[16] separately. Thus we have sight, hearing, taste, smell, balance, pheromones, touch, each sense participating in the process with sums of values linked to myriad appearances deconstructed. The kind of value would be relative such as fast, slow, lots, little and so on but mainly separated out by being a specific sort of value linked to specific deconstructions. The value of it would be relative to having whatever deconstruct and value was relevant to experience, which is what Maxwell's demon does, turns warm water, say, into hot and cold water. Why does the demon epicentre 'want' all the fast, hot, molecules in one place? Because this provides hot, by putting the same values in one place we create a quality, hot, which was not there before in the same way but was nevertheless relative, i.e. warm, between hot and cold. So shuffling values around and relating them differently can create quantitative value, temperature linked to qualitative appearances, hot. If the values are all around, being able to shuffle them about can bring about new relationships and thus link qualities to quantities differently. If the relationship becomes cleaned up as order for us then we can manipulate the dialectical process to harvest experience in specific ways so that qualities and quantities are related for us rather than only contingently as if we simply rooted and grew from blood and soil. We call this intelligence using the word to point at the art of linking quantity and quality, which is essentially what our nervous system does because it can shift from part/pattern to part/whole, a contextual manipulation using the body.

---

[16] Dietrich A

What we need to have, if we are to get to some understanding of how phenomena emerge from our processing is some idea of how phenomena appear to us from experience. If we think about an apple for example we would have to already know what an apple is like, what it is used for, what kind of relationships it gives rise to for us, in shops for example, in pies, as a nick name for a town. All of these relationships are produced it seems, to order by us reading about them as we do on the pages here, and then having to produce them using our hands and brains. If we went out to find an apple we would have to produce them in our hands. If we were in an orchard of apple trees we may, if the season is right, find an apple that actually appears to us on a tree. If we see an apple in front of us, and then turn our back the apple will still be there when we turn back around again, unless someone is playing a trick on us. Hiding apples is not something that experience does to us unless it is with night, the covering of leaves in a surprising way, by seasonal change, by torrential rain or heavy snow, fog, sudden blindness, a stroke, and all of these are possible, yet usually the apple will repeat itself as pure movement until it drops, rots, becomes a new apple tree, or is eaten and digested, perhaps. Once eaten the same apple cannot be undigested and put back on the tree as it was. It is forever changed however a new apple remarkably like the first, but different, takes its place in the orchard, not now but as the year replicates itself, and there will in all probability be a next year unless the orchard owner sells out to a developer of housing estates, for example, or if there is an earthquake that destroys the land. But in our world of transcendental workers we have new resources, books, that tell us about apples that do not need the experiences outlined above. This short paragraph supplements many years' experience of apples using text, the phenomena used in transcendental work that grew exponentially after the 6th century BN [before now][17].

What we have just experienced, what I wanted you to read, is the proposition that the process we are makes phenomena appear to us based on what appeared to us as experience and now appears as an experience of the dialectic which produces the phenomenon. Thus we refine the phenomenon from appearances and also the construct which is the mass value of experience. This is why we now have boys and girls in urban space who know what eggs are but not where they come from since the blood and soil is lost to them. Blood and soil workers learn about grain, seeds, eggs, sex, harvest and crop failure. Note that the way in which phenomena appear relies upon the dialectical processing of what appears to us prior to processing but cannot do so once it has already appeared. The resources are different. The apple, seed, tree and seasons for example are different in text experience than in soil experience. The former is delimited the latter limited in practice to the earth. In the former the apple can be New York, the big apple, but in the latter in a pie or in text but not imagined. I will rapidly move on to processes because imagination refers to our ability to delimit our harvesting of experience but we can do this by exploring what is limited as well as what is unlimited. It is however an extrapolation of what has appeared to us processed into phenomena that we can make use of and exchange for appearances in the scheme of things that we gradually accumulate as what we call assets, what we will call

---

[17] But has been amongst us since the 7th millennium BN

the commodities. The phenomena are in part values and deconstructed appearances shuffled around repetitively and centripetally or centrifugally to create epicentres and patterns with values attached to part/pattern relationships that provide contexts that then provide the basis for deductive reasoning. If we accept that dialectic processing becomes causal as to order or entropy so that experience is actually altered by it then we can appreciate that new value/appearance relationships are created as phenomena of different kinds. A single cell can be altered by the movements relating to what we call media, different sorts of value/appearance relationships all of which are ultimately made from pure movement having relative differences in how those movements play out as values in contingent yet contextual relationships. These alterations to the nervous system will be examined in a rather vulgar way in the following chapters, meaning that you don't have to be a brain surgeon to follow the argument.

To recap on this chapter then: the term **sui-generis** refers to the concept of nothing out of which all movement emerges. Some movements regenerate or repeat, we do not always know how, and these can vary in the amount of time they take to do so and create the appearance of space. Qualities that appear to us as time and space are the same sorts of relationships because they have contingent quantitative values that are shuffled into quantitative part/pattern relationships that alter the dialectic actions leading to function or lack of function. Thus we may or may not learn to replicate part/pattern relationships of value/appearance on an individual or socialised basis because we reconstruct what is again deconstructed. If we go back for a meal in a restaurant we don't always like it as much as we did the first time we ate in it.

It is possible to conjecture that if something happens to us then it is possible that it may happen to others and vice versa. So that if I accommodate an apple and can then reproduce a recollection of it, then any other one of us might be able to do so as well. In addition if we meet up well away from any apples but in the same experiences, sharing the same, or almost the same beginning, the two of us, for there are now two, can recollect apple and can exchange the recollection in a way that realises the apples are possibly similar but also perhaps not the same, thus tasty to eat if ripe, sour if unripe, red or perhaps yellow, on trees, in bowls, in shops, possibly in salads but hardly ever on heads with arrows being shot at them. If we understand this as a lot of shuffling of values relative to qualities superfast we begin to get the hang of it. Apples on heads with arrows rely upon the harvesting of William Tell stories that may or not be shared in the nothing of the meeting, and some people do not like apples.

The next few chapters will show how in a vulgar way [rather than a sophisticated neuro-scientific way] we can easily understand how such an amazing ability is fairly common to all human beings, potentially at least once we get a handle on this concept of sui generis as movement held motionless, and then being able to replicate the outcomes of letting movement happen using assets that may or may not include particular harvests, of relative experiences that have seemingly happened to us before. I think the important point will be that we can replicate what we have learnt, mastered, even when we are in, as we must be, other relationships, thus we get the sense of being able to control what we do, the processing, so as to create order, be it limited or unlimited labour. We seem able to act like little recorder/players but there is no guarantee that what is recorded and thus harvested as an individual provides us all with the resources required so that we can play the same experience again and again. In fact that seems impossible and yet rationality and instrumentalism depend upon that delusion. Nothing is the only truth, if you need one.

Chapter Two
Symbiosis

Diagram 2.1 The Emergent Construct

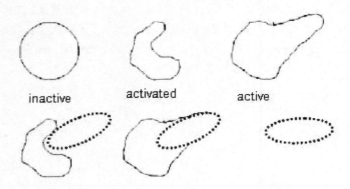

inactive   activated   active

I am going to call the accumulation of experience the construct because I need to establish that it is a mass value even though it receives the results of more or less continuous movements by way of the arrival of appearances that are the result of accommodations emerging from sui generis that is the permanent nothingness, the starting point of all movement and thus of all experience, every value that we feel and every appearance that we sense. This divergence of value and appearance is seminal to our nervous system[18].

The construct is the constant mass of experience the body has acquired from its condition of living. The construct is constantly

---

[18] Dietrich A

adjusted by more and various shunting around of values and appearances delivered from sui generis to the senses, and thence to myriad epicentres of action that keep us alive and relative to contexts as they happen. The nervous system deconstructs appearances but we argue they are accumulated as the construct or mass value/appearance relationship in the context of the body. Sui generis is our universal part of nothingness which places us in the context of movements according to their appearance to us individually. The accumulation of appearances relative to each individual who senses them, is stored as value/appearance relationships in which the appearances are deconstructed. These appearances produce chemical and electrical changes correlated to values within the body relating to processes that keep us alive and relate us to contexts. Thus the relationships between appearances and actions become reflexively connected up contextually so that they are born and live or die. The only effective control we have as individuals is to extrapolate the extent of the context/s that is/are happening to the part we currently process as a phenomenon.

The actual relationship we have relies upon our individual ability to carry around, as a mass such as the snail carries a shell that is and yet is also becoming, growing, the construct that is the mass of experience received from our own unique sui generis and also the processing we do. Because many movements are seemingly replicated, so that for example there are lots of us, and say, lots of trees, and lots of days, we often share similar experiences, contexts and appearances in the process, the subject of this chapter. If cells are given values by accommodating appearances out of sui generis, and then convey those values as chemical and electrical changes to myriad parts of the body, that then alter or as we may say appear to control those chemical and electrical changes, then we have an interactive system, which is what we are individually and as a race relative to sui generis and experience of it. In other words if an apple activates cells when we see it eaten and we can act to put an apple into our mouths then we may eat apples. If they are good to eat we can, using the same system, become reflexive as to eating good to eat apples. Given that we appear, with more or less success, to be able to achieve such feats it remains only for the neuro scientists to tell us how, exactly, we can do this, which they cannot do at the moment. A few decent contributions on this are included in the appendix, by the way. Needless to add, perhaps, notice that an actual apple is not reproduced at any point inside the nervous system, nor is it, we argue, necessary to have anything other than an initial appearance of an apple like appearance to provide the chemical electrical changes to our nervous systems. The first apple eater made a creative leap that did not kill her, or him. Of course in this account of symbiosis, all sui generis is unique, even if the apple emerging from it appears to be the same the experience is different.

Differences, we might expect, become less appreciated as the same apple repeats its appearance. Symbiosis seems to include the notion that what has appeared is now, as we say, accumulated and has acquired a reflexive passage through the nervous system as a deconstructed appearance each with values equally widely distributed yet appearing to us as an apple, as being eaten by what appears as one of us, as being relished as refreshing, and tasty or bitter, and ready or not yet ready for eating. Symbiosis is this accommodation of appearances and the accumulation of experience in which not only appearances of apples but the value of deconstructed apples as form and value become reflexively established in some way. But these are not simply retrieved. Note that the context is contemporaneously experienced and because sui-generis is unique, the apple is not experienced on its own but in the context of a changing milieu.

In order to conjecture what appears as the appearance in context we need to have a way of matching part/pattern relationships as they happen. Our bodies seem to have this by way of the massive number of locations in the neural system and the parallel causal chains set in motion by any appearances. For our purposes here all we need to believe is that appearances that emerge from sui generis are deconstructed and shunted around or along quite a few, neural passages until they can be left somewhere ready to be shunted along again when the relative conditions are propitious, which would be when, for example, we are hungry in an apple orchard, or trying to work out what sort of fruit pie to have for dinner. The part played by symbiosis as a short hand to our understanding of the process we all use, is to accommodate, accumulate and then assimilate these appearances and these values. The exact details must be left to ongoing research but we need to grasp the principle that epicentres of storage of deconstructed appearance and value measurements allow diverse appearances and diverse values to accumulate contextually, in other words relatively to part/pattern relationships, limited only by what appears to us and our having the necessary neural resources.

We are in the fortunate position of not having to declare which part of the neural system is able carry out this process, only that we do seem to have this ability and thus must have such a neural system. Thus we are able to accommodate, as I am calling it, an apple, that plays its movement to us all the while playing us, activating us, and our nervous system is played and adjusts itself in such a way that an apple is deconstructed via smell, sight and perhaps touch by way of accumulation. These accumulations do not go away, they remain and become part of what I am calling a mass construct that is the continuous total effect of what the individual has seen, smelled and touched again and again. The apple is an epicentre of movement that was a seed, then a tree, and then a flower and now an apple. The individual can move away from the apple and still be the individual who has seen smelled and touched an apple. With practice and with widely varying results we know that we are able mutatis mutandis, all things being equal, to remember, as we call it, the sight, smell, and touch of an apple and of different apples from different orchards.

The construct then, is an epicentric concept, which means that the actual accumulation is massively fragmented in time and space, as we understand them, but is as if it resides in one location in the body since that is the accounting balance of the sum total of accumulation and relies on the dialectic between the construct as a resource of accommodation and sui generis as a resource of milieu. A wiring metaphor is quite useful as a description of the way any measure of value within a cell, be it analogue or metric[19], is transferred within the nervous system to many sites of consequence responsible for accumulating the experience as storage and also as a change in value that matters. That wiring shows nothing but wet connections with a propensity to becoming as if wired by a complex developmental process that is unique but common to all of us or we could say analogue in context and at the same time metric individually. The sheer number of such connections in use is more than the number of grains of sand on Earth which is why we find differences between individuals even when the overall appearance inside each body is not dissimilar if we take out the nervous system and have a look at it, which in principle we can do using a scan. A total account of all those connections would satisfy those who wish to identify material conditions, measured, metric, but this remains impossible for all practical and even wildly impractical purposes, the number of cells is too great and the individual differences make it even less plausible, plus as we shall see the flow of chemical change varies at any cell making the total number of conditions impossible for any counting to occur, thus sui-generis is the only possible metric truth which is nothing. Analogue truth depends upon the milieu, which is unique.

Diagram 2:2 shows the complexity of our visual mechanism.

---

[19] The reference to analogue and metric is so as to note that whilst some values are useful merely as measures of amount of chemical or electrical quantities the use of value can also be part of an analogue relationship that when combined gives rise to some quality such as hot or cold for example which may or may not be felt by us so as to be accurately valued and yet actually have a specific value in cells of the nervous system at all times..

Diagram 2:2. The complexity of our visual mechanism

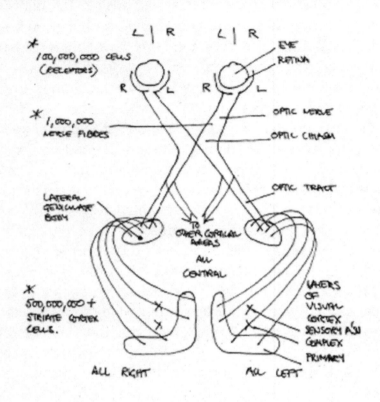

We must all come to understand that while we each may have a similar visual mechanism the chemical and electrical interactions of the nervous system make each individual construct, accumulation of experience, different and each wiring diagram different at the neural scale so that whilst two individuals may share the same diagram 2.2 they will have very different neural values spread around the body. The differences in wiring diagrams might reasonably be thought of as less different between individuals than the differences in the construct, the mass value, since experiences are unique to the individual whereas the wiring installation depends on the instructions given by DNA which to that extent is the epicentre of the phenotype, the individual of each species.

Note that the basic mechanism at work in the nervous system of the human body is a single cell of the sort illustrated in the diagram 2:3.

Diagram 2:3. A simplified drawing of a single nerve cell

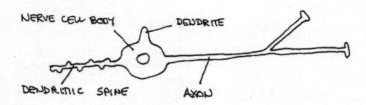

Each cell or neuron can produce many of the wet connections shown in diagram 2.4 across which chemical change takes place giving us the concept of hard wiring we have already mentioned. Note that the point at which each cell connects to each other cell shown in diagram 2:4 experiences the speed and volume of what we might call change in value which is whether or not the cell is active or inactive, firing or not firing an electric pulse through the axon to make neural transmitters that activate other cells through the dendrite across the synaptic cleft.

Diagram 2:4. A simplified drawing of a dendritic connection

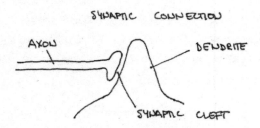

Diagram 2:5 the varying speed and volume of chemical change

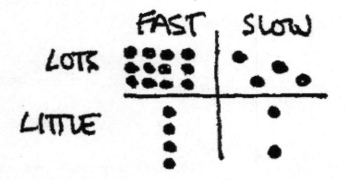

Remember that any change in the construct, as a resource of accumulated appearances is, epicentric, i.e., is actually deconstructed and spread around all over the body, emerges from sui-generis since the body is part of sui-generis, and so prompts consequences unique to each of us yet having correlations with our innate ability to experience these consequences and relate them to context. In diagram 2:5 we can see that the change is not only on or off but slow and minimal or fast and significant, or we could say absent, casual, slight or urgent and as we have seen inactive or active. In addition the tipping point[20] for passing on change could be called a potential for emergence out of sui-generis in every single cell who is analogously a voter for some action or inaction.

This is a point that is missed out of any purely mechanical version of our nervous system and it is certainly excluded from descriptions of behaviours that have already arrived at deductive functionality and common usage as mere extrapolations, working models of a whole series of reproductive actions and experimental actions. The timing of the adjustments in the plural passages shunting these changes around can be varied so that circuits can be put to use that eventually cut off other circuits in a complex synchronisation, a sequence of tipping points and passages, producing an overall behavioural relationship that has through this process acquired the appearance of functionality. Just as the 25 frames per second of a film relies upon the light passing through it so the movement that never moves provides the baseline for all possible scales, speeds, amounts and directions of movement. The movements are fast, slow, this or that way, along this or that corridor of neurons, just like a complex transport system having a daily timetable once the nervous system becomes more and more reflexive.

The difficulty for us seems to be that the body's ability to hold on to values as mass experience, albeit epicentrically described as a construct, mass experience, is such that actual

---

[20] Calvin W H

values are consequences of movements that emerge from sui generis all the time, unceasingly. Thus what we have is relative movements that are caught up in all movements which is the context in which we experience them. The question we have to ask is what makes the body able to alter those movements in which it is caught up so as to survive or become functional, which is almost but not quite the same effect? This requires the counterpoint of experience, what I call synergy, the other half of the individual's dialectic with sui-generis' production of appearances processed as symbiosis accumulating and assimilating, which is what I describe as synergy in the next chapter [3].

Chapter Three:

Synergy

I have used the term symbiosis to suggest that accumulated appearances become, epicentric as an apparent location of what emerges from sui-generis so what is spread around produces consequences that are unique to each of us yet have correlations between us in terms of our innate ability to experience these consequences as if located relatively. This makes meaning possible but at the cost of fixing part/pattern relationships. The changes that occur because of symbiosis are not only on or off but also slow and minimal or fast and significant, or we could say absent, casual, slight or urgent and as we have seen inactive or active, on or off. In addition there are tipping points for change that could be called a potentiality for change. This indicates two conditions, a propensity of some sort and a more accurate yet temporary set of values which are widely dispersed even though appearing to be located. Synergy is my term for what these potentialities and appearances produce such that epicentres become apparent such as a set of phenomena including an acting body. I am not sure if thought is part of this or part of incorporation that I treat in the next chapter.

Symbiosis is the dialectic between sui-generis and existence that produces the construct as a mass experience of accommodations that have been assimilated as the process continues by living day by day aided by what we refer to as the circadian clock adjusting body mechanisms to day and night time uses. Symbiosis includes the production of values related to staying alive and functioning but some other process is needed in order to direct the consequences of symbiosis towards the actions that are necessary for this. Some call this dynamic homeostasis although there are, in addition, other sorts of relationships that are not entirely those required for survival as such in that they come to us, or we to them, and adopt them as useful to us individually and in groups.

Synergy is my term for our creation, what is made in terms of action or process, such that appearances appear to us and it has become philosophically commonplace to call these appearances phenomena. It is a philosophical issue to attempt and even succeed to make lists of all the various categories of movement that go to make up one appearance and of course synergy is creating an appearance based on previously experienced deconstructions of what appears to us. The original appearance for experience is as any part of a context that appears. Synergy is my term for a refining process that feeds forward, since it cannot go back, into symbiosis so that patterns become epicentric within a context that becomes the edge of phenomena.

Whereas we know quite well amongst us that the movement of an apple is contained within itself for now, whereas some months before it was a flower, before that a branch and so on. We also know that the epicentre of those changes is in truth DNA participating in the centripetal coming together of resources such as nutrients and water. The apple that this synergy creates out of the construct as a resource is contemporaneous with symbiosis continuing its work so that the dialectic between sui-generis and symbiosis is complemented by synergy to the extent that, for example when sleeping, synergy is able to make phenomena appear with no assistance from contemporary symbiosis other than that of the body that is sleeping and perhaps some extraneous appearances or lack of them. The dialectic appears to be, now, that of the body, even though the body has become the epicentric source of the appearance that in effect combines that of symbiosis with that of synergy to provide phenomena as they appear to us. I am suggesting that rather than see from outside the body we see using resources both in and around the body in a complex way that we are still not yet clear about in terms of neuroscience. Nonetheless, in spite of this lack of clarity, it seems clear that we do not see in what some call the Cartesian sense of a distal, source, and proximal, sensed, image. It is known to be more complex than that; the processing is not that of a camera and a digital image.

When we look at the visual system we have, for which see diagram 2.2 above, we see that the complexity is such that many parts go to make up what we consider to be a phenomenon such as an apple, its shape, colour, there are outlines, considerations of volume, size, distance, proximity, smell maybe, then touch and as we progress we find that these are broken down into smaller and smaller parts all of which become pure movement along more diverse parts of the many processes including relationships with for example taste and/or eating contexts that have been experienced in some way, perhaps not necessarily by eating an apple. It will be necessary for neurosurgeons struggling with the workings of our nervous systems to become more familiar with the biological processing but not for us since we are interested in the way the whole process works so as to let us know what is happening. We need a way to link context to some kind of coping mechanism if we can, otherwise we remain dysfunctional because rational and thus deductive interactions rely upon some sort of bounded relationship that can be produced, like a map, for example, that can be altered at will so as to make it more accurate or more inclusive or exclusive and so on.

Symbiosis accommodates, assimilates and accumulates experience as noise whilst synergy uses experience as a resource and refines it as feed forward processing so that phenomena emerge out of noise. Note well, that all appearances emerge out of sui-generis including those we say are part of synergy. Synergy is that part of the dialectical process that presents to symbiosis by hand and brain, both of these, and it makes it very difficult for us to distinguish exactly which is which although it is a refining process so that we get close to it. Essentially synergy has the input from the body whereas symbiosis has the input from the body and all else. Experience is limited yet emerges from what has no limits, sui-generis. Sui-generis has no limits and yet provides only limited experience to each body. Each body is limited to what it is rather than what it is not. The refinement of noise is therefore imperfect and yet impressive and can result in quite accurate hand-brain coordination such as finding apples and eating them.

At the moment we are at that point, describing what synergy must be like, which is the involvement in the process that draws on experience adding those influences over the process that have accumulated through the experiences of each individual. The construct is the mass experience containing all that has been accumulated, assimilated and accommodated, in that order whereas symbiosis is the opposite process of accommodation, assimilation and accumulation. We know that there are aleatory and subliminal influences over the process that emerge from sui-generis but do not appear to us yet are assimilated and accumulate in the processing and thus from the construct as if experience and/or as first time appearances on their way to the construct.

The process is a constant process even when asleep that seems to be centred within us which together with our refined phenomena make it seem that we act upon phenomena as a body acting as we do and to a great extent that does emerge as functional behaviour. Synergy is the dialectical part of the process which I am claiming produces feelings because it is the processing of myriad values as they precipitate action by altering the process so as to maintain part/pattern relationships that have acquired meaning by the limiting effects of refinements that are successful in producing functional action since to remain unlimited is to reduce deduction as a possibility. This processing is so quick, so fast, that we believe we are responding as individuals but this is the effect of epigenesis, the bringing into being of an epicentred locus of apparent control as the process attempts to refine appearances into phenomena and thus also contexts.

We gain an understanding, i.e. a functional articulation of what happened at the cost of giving up the unlimited noise as synergy allows the emergence of an extrapolation that provides us with a meaningful context within which we appear to act as functional or what we call rational beings. Synergy allows us to accommodate differently, exploring in common using symbiosis, which all the while is processed by synergy introducing the potential for individual refinements and expressions of function. The effect is to vacillate between limited and unlimited resources, repeating experience, accommodating by trial and error until a set of phenomena become acted upon in common if a group, or acted upon by an individual if alone.

It appears that the daily labours of this processing undergoes assimilation during times of sleeping such that the dialectical process, the whirl of movements of the day, consolidate themselves as shown in diagram 3.1 –

Diagram 3.1 The Consolidation Process

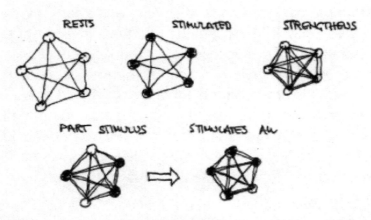

What I have called extrapolation, controlled articulation of phenomena out of the process, is difficult because sui-generis is indifferent to location whereas the processing produces this epicentric emergence out of it. Unlike the assumption that the body is, as stated above, an epicentre of action, we are taught to believe we have control over the process so that we decide what to extrapolate but I am arguing that this cannot be true since we do not exist except as the epicentric part of the extrapolation, in other words we make ourselves up ourselves based on vicarious trial and error processing. The result of this vicarious processing may well be almost exactly similar to saying there is a person, just as we say, for example the sun rises when it does not, however the insistence of our ancestors in some inner being has created enormous stress because we have tended to look for him or her all our lives and they do not exist as beings but as process. Thus we do not change our minds but the process alters the extrapolations we act upon, including thinking them, according to influences that are sometimes known to us and at other times not.

For the moment I am calling extrapolations metric and analogue because they are either phenomena or process. These definitions have to be taken as process based so that whenever we say that we feel anger, or a vague idea that a chair is comfortable that is analogue and metric according to context. The chair can be measured using a measure and the comfort is measured using analogue values that cannot be shared or fixed. If we do fix them it becomes metric and to alter an adage, we decide on our chair and have to sit on it. The contemporary insistence on excellence and perfection that took off 2.5K years before now with such vigour in the western world as science, destroys this subtlety and is responsible, in my opinion, for much of the poverty of global political economic wisdom because it is searching for an ideal, which is vague like the grail, but having to measure its success against a metric outcome, which is capable of perfection but completely open to a zillion interpretations by a global population on a daily basis. The diagram below illustrates this:

Diagram 3.2. The analogue/metric paradox

The basic concept of Smile as a title is this rictus grin of the delusional totalitarian link between ideal and utopia that transcends all the processing hanging from it in the erroneous belief that utter functionality has been achieved. The fact that we do however have and share such delusions with enormous enthusiasm points to an ability to not only vicariously explore noise but to refine it into extrapolations linking hand and brain in feedback towards actuality and propensity that relies upon the very unreliability of the ideal to be made utopian or the utopian to be found ideal. I call our ability to incorporate either of these two, propensity and actuality, and join them functionally in extrapolations, acting upon them and thus altering what we produce as ideal and as utopian, is what we explore in the next chapter. The drive towards functionality and thus in effect towards identity and value is both cause and satisfaction of the processing which has both without the need for any such drive since identity and value emerge as phenomena with values if we wait for this to happen on its own accord as a part of the process which we are not able to resist since we do not exist to resist it. It is the delusion that we exist as a thing not of our own creation but of some grand whole of which we are part, which provides the delusion that we must labour to fit function rather than experience.

Chapter Four

Incorporation

Whose Context?

Diagram 4.1: The Contextual Shift

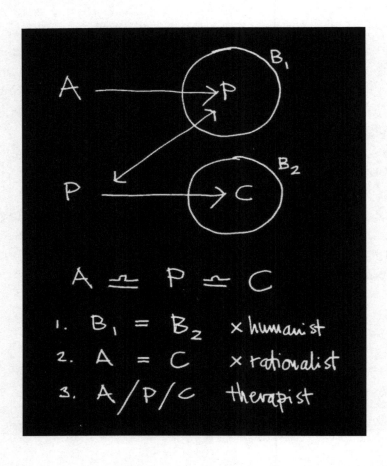

In the diagram 4.1 above, B1 represents the context experienced by the individual [phenotype] whilst B2 represents the transcendental context that cannot be experienced by one individual since it is in what some call the social arena or the space and time of the social[21] [genotype]. Since sui-generis is the bottom and empty line of all movement it is impossible to determine the context in either case. Thus the more B2 is assumed to be genotypically the context the less exactly it correlates to the context that is B1, the one experienced by the phenotype, the individual, the particular and specific. Again we must note and realize that since the context is epicentric to experience it is ignorant of many movements emergent from sui-generis and will remain so as a condition of experience.

The point is that the individual experiences B1 whereas the individual must also allow for B2 or run the risk of offending others like themselves since all are genotypes, all individuals are human by fact of birth and life. The epicentre that we refer to as individual can move relative to other epicentres that we call surroundings and as an inclusive term, context, in order to become and remain reasonably functional and he or she can explore the work of symbiosis and synergy as it happens. This exploration and response to feedback from exploration is what I call incorporation.

B1 as a phenomenon produced from incorporation, this dialectic between potentiality and actuality as experienced on a daily basis, has the epicentre of the individual as its probable location, domicile, even though that focus is always set in the peripheral circumference that changes with the movement of

---

[21] Arendt H

the individual by hand and brain. That is to say that both activations of hand and brain may alter the periphery and thus require an alteration of the focus. The model of this sort of exploration is demonstrated in a vulgar way below in diagram 4.2.

Diagram 4.2. Vulgar Model of Exploring Time and Space

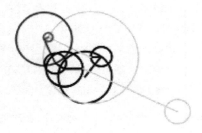

The movement emerging from sui-generis moves from focus to periphery as a basic means of establishing the part/pattern relationship[22]. With each peripheral halting there is the new focal point and a new beginning for a periphery. Each periphery alerts myriad other cells via the network, the controlling factors being the gradual establishment of corridors, passages as we have said that corrupt this entirely open process into the business of living as a phenotype. An asset for living emerges as we see in the genotype with individual variations that are more propensities than certainties at the level of some activations and more certain that not in others. Activations are inevitable, propensities are variable.

---

[22] McGilchrist I

The term <u>incorporation</u> then is used to represent the labouring part of what is happening that seemingly determines the asset and its expenditure of energy leading eventually to a working relationship with other assets. Thus the body becomes an asset of its environment and the environment as asset of a body. The environment is an epicentre created by the spherical nature of the earth upon which we live and the phenomena within a context produced by the dialectic between symbiosis and synergy and the additional process of incorporation. That process has an epicentre in what emerges as a relationship that becomes functional, including the joint asset of a body with certain propensities and an environment that complements those propensities making a joint asset which we have been inclined to refer to as a culture. I would prefer to call cultural that which is described in the chapter which follows, solidarity, since that transcends incorporation so that functional advantages, if they exist, become an asset that can only be produced by the combination of epicentres into a coherent group.

The point is that it is not a simple process of an analysis of incoming sensations and processing because there is no analyser as such other than a process. Once we become robots or ants, as some scientists claim[23] then we become the phenomenon of the analysis whereas we are an epiphenomenon of the exploratory process of incorporation. Although none of us can explain how this process operates exactly[24] this exegesis offers an explanation of how we can

---

[23] Wilson E O
[24] Fodor. J

begin to have a conversation about it without inventing spiritual causes that then have to be explained or else take their place on a metaphysical edge to exploration, which is the subject of the planned third volume in the trilogy of which this book is the first.

We do of course share many reflexive interactions that DNA replicates in all of us if possible so that, for example, we screw up our eyes so as to push eyeballs back into sockets to avoid damage when suddenly hit in the face. We know these reflexes are innate to the human condition, the genotype, but examples such as this are very few compared to the infinite range of social and cultural behaviours that follow the same pattern, appearance, sense, process, output, but rely not on one robotic model but on an infinite number of all possible combinations. The confusion has been over the fact that on any one day there are, let us say, over five thousand languages and thus at least that many cultures, within which many of us appear as masters of those languages and cultures and to a great degree robotic within that language or culture. It is an amazing feature of our race that we become reflexive within B1 to such an extent that B2 emerges as to all intents and purposes identical since it is measured in the metric zone of diagram 3.2 and cannot be measured in B1 other than as an analogue measurement by each and every individual. The epiphenomenon that is the individual, working with the epiphenomenon that is the context B2 thus produce the epiphenomenon that is B3, what I call the cultural context. What we have rehearsed thus far in this text is that as well as B1 there are B2's and B3's that represent the context of individual, social and cultural exploration and functionality such that social interaction and individual interaction can be related to a third cultural epiphenomenon that transcends both individual and social incorporation to provide functionality and the emergence of assets and actions relative to them entirely reliant on reflexive action by hand and brain of each and every participating individual. Diagram 4.2 shows the three contextual relationships.

Diagram 4.3. <u>The Three Contextual Epiphenomena</u>

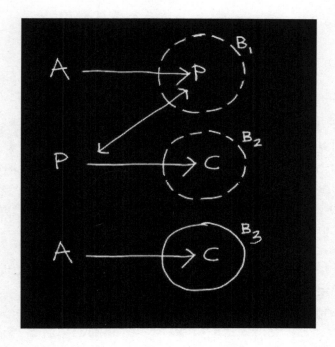

B1 is limitless or limited according to the exploration of the individual that I have referred to as labouring. B3 is limited by the absolute need to be reflexive [robotic] within all contexts that allow what we shall call a membership or solidarity as in chapter five below, which may be regarding B2 or B3. B2 represents many relationships to context but allows that shift from B1, personal, to B2, social, that provides the limited yet limitless and fecund ground, in both limited and limitless applications, for B3 to emerge as a product of our labours be it creative or as apprentices or as the sustained actions of masters of that specific culture.

We can see in diagram 4.1 at the start of this chapter, that

i.   We may assume [wrongly] that all B1's are B2's.

and

ii.   We may alternatively assume [wrongly] that all A's are reflexively connected to specific P's within B2.

When we are taught to believe that processing is a straightforward kind of processing, an either or, we have no option but to invent good and bad as spiritual causes that we must then find out about or place as limits to our exploration as if answers to our labours. This must also be accompanied by a belief in luck or destiny which is of course inevitably what we find in every example of spiritual culture. the difficulties with this are the subject of the second volume in my trilogy, laugh out loud, LOL, so we will not treat them here, merely note that this book allows a conversation in which the spiritual is not required, is not called upon to explain life and its outcomes since that is not the question. We do not need to know the meaning of life merely to live it. We shall arrive at a point in my work in which we note that we ought not to treat other individuals as assets without their cooperation and agreement. The reason for this is so that we take advantage of their individuality and thus their openness to life itself. This does not lend itself to any rapid accumulation of assets nor to any rapid mastery of what emerges out of sui-generis. At times individuals become assets by default because what emerges engulfs them and accumulation overcomes them with rapacious actions for which we obviously have a propensity. Such cases require our attention since they are dysfunctional. One of humanities current problems seems to be that we feel such rapacious actions are laudable rather than worrying and in need of therapy, mainly because we attribute good and bad to spiritual causes rather than to what appears to us processed as experiences in which we ought to be open to labour over incorporation and are not allowed to do so.

Before moving on to solidarity, which is the term I use to describe the transcendental context epicentric to incorporation by individuals and groups, the culture as a phenomenon, I want to confirm the dialectic of symbiosis and synergy that we all share. Diagram 4.4 shows the eyeball and diagram 4.5 shows a slice of the retina at the back of the eyeball. Any appearances we accommodate, in this case by the eye, is significantly altered by many parts of the body before it becomes a phenomenon for us notwithstanding the point that the cells shown in the diagrams 4.4 and 4.5 are related in a complex way to the passage of energy that light is when entering the eyeball. Thus while the epicentre that is the person may be aware of moving the eye the body meanwhile acts in ways with which we are unaware in the epicentred context of the individual that we believe ourselves to be, until now that is. Now that we are aware of our process basis, in which we are ineluctably immersed, we can see in diagram 4.5 that what we believe to be valuations of energy are placed in a location furthest from the incoming image. In front of the most sensitive cells of measurement are cells that modify and alter valuations so that we may note the processing commences at the very threshold of what we call perception.

Diagram 4.4 The human eyeball in section

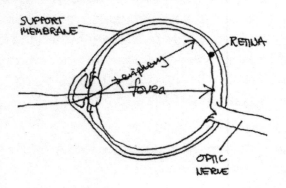

Diagram 4.5 Some of the cells in the retina of the eye

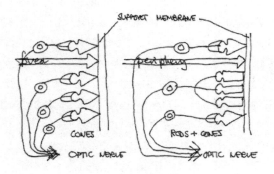

The illusion is, as we say of both an actor responding and of a conditioned wiring diagram [of great complexity][25] and that illusion may be so strong as to delude us into making do with the outcome that processing has presented to us, made reflexive, created as an asset combining container and contained, leading us to the inevitable conclusion that the epicentre of our experience is that of being an actor, or that of responding to social and cultural imperatives, rather than processing appearances as they happen in a specific yet not always experienced or anticipated context[26].

Proof of the correlation of one to the other can be obtained insofar as such proof can be dialectically maintained by happenings repeating contextually and sequentially thus continuing the illusion of an actor performing functionally within some container, thus reinforcing the illusion. But these may be any one of provisional B1's, B2's and B3's as contexts serving to encourage the propensities influencing the epicentric phenomena that are part/pattern as individual, social, cultural and of course phenomenological also, the emergence of even one phenomenon being exactly the same process and yet relative to the other epicentric phenomena.

The nervous system is not so much fixed as developed or conditioned so that it becomes reflexive according to rules relating to the **dialectical incorporation** which is to say fixed as behaviours that work, are successful in bringing the various

---

[25] Plotkin H

[26] Those who are unconvinced are invited to read **any** of the popular works on neuroscience listed in the appendix and they will find how necessary it is to begin this conversation without spiritual cause being any part of it

epicentres into functioning relationships as extrapolations of both hand and brain that we have grown to reference as ideal and utopian, those that are qualitative and quantitative. These definitions lead to beliefs in internal and external relationships that confuse us, which are discussed in the second volume LOL as I have shown, above. Our relationship is to processing and our propensity to produce phenomena such that the processing itself becomes essential to a functionality that seeks to relate all phenomena quantitatively, which is not possible. As much as we may labour to find a part/whole relationship within which every action is deductive it is a never ending struggle and an impossible condition which is why we refer to it as utopia. This desire for utopia incorporates our propensity for idealism and we are corrupted the more the two transcend the labouring of experience. This is the basis of the title Smile, the totalising rod of the utopian-ideal acting as a condition of processing by making it reflexive and thus unresponsive to all that emerges from sui-generis.

Diagram 4.6 The Smile

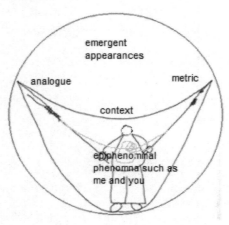

Chapter Five:
Solidarity

Fixing Processing – the drive to the end of experience – the drive to death - function

We can argue that incorporation takes time to arrive at any correlation, reflexively useful or otherwise, between processing and experience so that a functional relationship between analogue and metric measures consolidates all our processing on certain relationships into an asset out of a dialectic relationship between construct and cosmology as it is in sui-generis between the epiphenomenon of the individual and the epiphenomenon of the earth or universe. Our incorporation converts labouring into functional relationships whenever certain epiphenomena appear as appearances, as they must, so that they participate in transcendental relationships between what have become for us pure and simple phenomena. This would be the ultimate socialisation since all social acts will be consolidated in such a processing practice. This is not to say that all social acts are consolidated in this or in any other way but that for us, in the incorporation in practice, in train, working rather than labouring over appearances, all actions by humans and the world are consolidated into the transcendental relationships between phenomena that have become totally reflexive within that process. When the nervous system is relatively free rather than reflexive as at birth, the clarity[27] as in the appearance of phenomena in place of noise, brought about by repetitious processing, helps to bring measured routines, functionality, to us more and more quickly the more we practice those functional proto-work labours. We convert them into what I call working practices.

Parents and guardians "looking after" having "found out" what works by coincidence and perhaps learning to repeat those coincidences socialise their children or perhaps fail to do so leaving the infants to learn for themselves, uncontrolled, unconditioned, unsocialised and thus perhaps particularly unique, still human, still genotypical, but without socialising reflexes. Because of the rapid onset of reflexive corridors within the nervous system, an essential part of becoming able to function, being able to work as a body, what is called developmental perception by some, the failure to socialise a child as to their humanity would seem to be catastrophic, we shall see how this is handled once we stop assuming that the newborn will get on with socialising itself which clearly it is not able to do on its own [sic]. By early years it seems that within the first few months certain passages become established that set the architecture of the nervous system in stone inasmuch as there is tracking of the otherwise untrodden snow of the new cells awaiting their calls to action so that they grow together axonally in the way that eventually all cells do having epicentres of responsibility towards the overall process of

---

[27] It is probably this clarity that made philosophers in the two centuries before now choose enlightenment as a concept rather than processing, at the same time perhaps placing an undue emphasis upon seeing rather than any other sensory category such as feeling, with the results we experience all around us now.

living in the world or a world that becomes known[28] to us. In the case of many animals the amount of free connectivity in the nervous system is far less [because there is], and in the case of insects for example it would appear that much of its nervous system is fixed as in a robotic relationship to appearances by way of connections that are more binary, on or off, than ambivalent as to on, off or "maybe". The extent of analogue time and space measures included in the process and made metric by incorporation is an important factor linked to what is licensed as acceptable levels of order/chaos during periods of growth and indeed adjustment as we struggle to unlimit the effects of growth so as to suit contemporary conditions of relativity in which we find ourselves, experience. Symbiosis and synergy will always determine the articulation of the body since symbiosis accommodates an appearance and synergy participates in the representation of those appearances but the speed at which that participation is delivered will clearly combine with sui-generis such that what is now will be with us before what is coming up to now and what has been is already lost to us. This situation which is living a life thus has its pressure without the need for any spiritual force other than the processing of a body that is immersed within a nothingness out of which emerges everything first as noise and then as phenomena that depend

---

[28] I can perhaps start using the word known to indicate a solidification of neural passageways that appears within our nervous systems making it difficult or impossible to resist as to the speed at which it can process compared to the lack of speed of other neural corridors yet to be opened up through exploration, yet to be reinforced, assimilated.

upon the very processing of which we have been unaware until now[29].

Functional outcomes rely on our individual processing, incorporation by the epicentre that is the individual, allowing us to believe and trust in any proof the process may find itself demanding such that the categories of phenomena that we refer to as time and space continue to allow functionality. Unfortunately the contributions from Freud and others over one hundred years ago, together with the cessation of labouring that has occurred within the professions, of all sorts, in favour of work, have socialised us into believing that there are more than one incorporator rather than that the one incorporation has to relate to however many appearances become processed, such that the transcendental outcome incorporates one or more primary epicentres that appear to influence what is being processed, experienced. I will discuss this more in the second and third volumes of the architecture of socialisation because that issue still engenders conversations of such magnitude amongst too many of us that even the remaining volumes in the trilogy will merely hint at the size of it. The very lives we lead amongst each other ensure that what we call certain knowledge carries with it a cost that is the lives and the freedoms of millions that will not stop until we

---

[29] The work of Freud and Jung and others did make a huge difference to our condition over one hundred years before now in the sense of showing us in the socialisation that cosmological and individual appearances have inserted into our processing without us having allowed for that fact until then – but we have had their contributions for over a century and done very little about it as a race that is humanity as a whole, we are still on our knees to spiritual forces, including contingency itself, rather than talking about the contributions people like Freud made to the architecture of socialisation which is the title of the trilogy.

learn more about ourselves, which is the point of this initial volume, to suggest how contributions already made can be incorporated more appropriately into what we do.

The dialectic that is the process, as that between experience and sui-generis as symbiosis and synergy, giving rise to phenomena, or between incorporation and the many possible epicentres of processing giving rise to transcendental relationships between phenomena, may mediate functionality to allow more or less time and this or that space according to values that themselves vary between analogue and metric values. The only way we can sense values is by way of appearances that the process articulates into a transcendental phenomenological model by way of a complex dialectic that is not only, potentially at least, between experience and everything else, but between many focal points and many peripheral contexts some of which will remain permeable allowing osmosis so that we may never have full certainty of the processing as to its ability to know everything, which is to say to convert all neural pathways into a neural network capable of responding to everything – the end of history as it is sometimes called. Incorporation reduces that everything to a scale that our processing can handle without becoming dysfunctional. Solidarity is our maintenance of that processing which we can only achieve by holding on to what is already incorporated such that the processing avoids labouring in favour of work at all times. Speedy processing of appearances to phenomena and speedy processing of behaviour to functioning relationships between everything, all phenomena, reinforces speedy processing, though not always the same speedy corridors, note. Thus solidarity is the same process for incorporation as an individual or as a group given only that in any group the individual must be related to it in some way that itself becomes processed as the transcendental phenomenological model in which the individual and others now believe they are as existing, whereas in fact they are still experiencing life, no more, no less, doubtless repressing life in order to maintain what is now the illusion of perfect functionality. We make life what we believe it to be in the transcendental phenomenological model just as the contributions by Kant and more recently by Hegel suggested but without the labours carried out even more recently by colleagues in the neurosciences and by some philosophers, most of whom remain unexplored by most of our race. We attempt to articulate processing in order to explore those relationships that appear to us transcendentally as phenomena rather than attempting the more difficult task of understanding the appearances themselves, which was the point of Husserl's contribution to this labour on the way to a more laborious study of the nervous system itself which continues today and is nowhere near complete.

It would be ludicrously and impossibly frustrating if each time we made a cup of coffee, or tea or filled a cup of water, we had to go through the whole process of accommodation, assimilation and rehearsal before we could sit down and enjoy it [although that is exactly what we do as children, strangers, inventors; we rehearse, learn and even acquire new approaches to articulaton and we encourage new appearances]. Happily the correlations needed to sustain the species lend themselves, it seems, to adaptive and improvisational uses for us so that as a species we have managed to evolve a wide range of platforms sharing many contexts so many groups with many incorporations sometimes called scripts or programmes, cultures[30], beliefs, ideologies, utopias and so on, gather together with many others seeking to define contexts of their own since boundaries are not set reflexively at birth to any great extent other than those in train because of DNA and its relationships to resources. The articulations that are incorporation often contradict each other leading to dissonance, individual and internecine strife including the now familiar and more interesting battles between the metaphysical border guards of meta-solidarities that we sometimes refer to as hegemonies or rules and so on.

Socialisation can become an important prompt for the conversion of work to labour and labour to work. The process I call solidarity forms passages and the part whole relationships between appearances and the incorporation of multiple centripetal requirements that co-exist within one rationalising boundary because appearances are processed to activate conditioned cells that produce phenomena of all sorts and the relationships are similarly produced. The commonality we appear to have between us is that phenomena appear in categories that are; time, space, analogue and metric in their transcendental phenomenological forms. Because I am using the transcendental phenomenological form now I will use the

---

[30] We should from now on understand cultures as "meta-solidarities" whose contextual edges are usually guarded by metaphysical phenomena of all sorts – see any book on religions of the world, or myth, for examples, or see the third of my trilogy, the metaphysical edge to be published in 2015

term platform although this may cause confusion with the term media, which is a similar category but I feel that many media may share a platform and mostly that is the case. Thus the platform will allow certain media to appear but not others and this becomes part of the solidarity. The socialisation should become even more obvious to the reader now. The fact that you are reading indicates that you share the transcendental phenomenological form of writing English, well or badly you may feel, the analogue case that I do not work to make overly metric by any means. You will what you call interpret all of what is written, if you read it all, and this is the illusion you use in order to arrive at your conclusion about my writing. But underneath the writing as the form of transcendental phenomena relating all these marks on paper or screen pixels and so on is the labouring I am hoping to stimulate in your incorporation that will allow you to process your experience differently. Your life is either gone or coming to you because sui-generis is now. Your so called history and future are other examples of the illusion provided by transcendental phenomenological models created for the purpose of relating epicentric appearances more or less according to the abilities of incorporation laboured over so that they become functional. Go to any art gallery or nursery and see how much labouring there is in producing any expression in any medium at all of any kind that becomes solid for any individual and often it will have become solid for others, friends, parents, even strangers incorporating experience in a similar way when they have the propensity to do so and so may.

Transitional periods, periods of adjustment, uncomfortable but often tolerable, emerge when this very limited sort of platform becomes very functional. We often say we belong to it, in spite of the fact that the process makes it, incorporates the appearances that bring phenomena to us on this platform along with us or we incorporate ourselves into the larger platform of social action and group action that sustains or promises to sustain our functionality whatever that may be so long as it does not fail to keep us alive in which case we would have to adapt or die, flee or fight, remove ourselves temporarily [in the transcendental phenomenological sense] or spatially [ditto]. Note well that the concept of moving the body belongs to the transcendental phenomenological model since the body cannot exist without us making it known to us in the dialectical process between experience and nothing that becomes everything. I have a concept called proto-work which is labouring towards functionality, the analogue/metric propensity in diagram 3.2., in chapter three. This makes synergy and for that matter symbiosis no panacea for human contentment or survival since what is value for some relies upon being outside what is value for others, stable as the proto-work necessities must become for us making social and group platforms uncomfortable at times and yet we can withstand, survive, an existence in them for a while at various levels of ambiguity [ambivalence and equivocation, the varying levels of analogue and metric value we experience because of what appears while on those platforms whether we realise there is a platform or not]. The most particular perhaps is the dialectic between value and incorporation in terms of making the proto-work necessities a common denominator for all persons or else using the labouring value of all to exploit as part of incorporation if we are aware of it as a process such that what we experience of improvisational theatre and game play is in probability the nearest some individuals ever get to experiencing at least the potential of incorporation as process. My contribution is simply to gather up the many contributions I have gathered up and labour over them to produce what appears here for you to read and consider. My own experience of improvisational acting confirms this contribution for me, that labouring over what otherwise appears scripted, and can appear scripted to others, and be part scripted part improvised, brings us close to the process of incorporation in the proto-work condition but in a way that is controlled, manageable, in the main, not always successful but nonetheless controlled. The same is the occurrence in childhood of similar potential but that is often accorded a place in the transcendental phenomenological model on many, many platforms such that childhood is historically a transitional period and thus over, in the past, not to be repeated rather than commonplace to us all our lives but suppressed, forbidden, to be avoided.

The previous chapter asks us to consider not the wiring diagram of the nervous system but the time taken for appearances out of nothing that could be anything and everything all at once to be accommodated and shifted to various locations within everything, assimilated in order to consolidate the construct as an asset within sui-generis as the resource drawn upon by synergy in its participation in the work of incorporation which is the necessary provision of phenomena these being the epiphenomena resulting from the epicentric conditions of appearances forcing values upon us given the immediacy of now. That construct can be consolidated, opened up or closed down, but not so fixed that it becomes actually solid since much of what is assimilated is not within the powers of articulation that each individual is able to contribute to that process. Consolidation may imply solidity but it will actually be a part/pattern situation just as much as any phenomenon is a part/pattern relationship that is epicentric to appearances giving rise to the appearance of a phenomenon rather than many or several and relating to other phenomena produced simultaneously and in strings or models and on platforms that I have described as the platform of solidarity with other incorporations who have individual processing but the same sort of powers over processing to enable correlations to emerge implying some form of conditioning fixed by incorporation, the prescience, coming to hand and brain of all phenomena for the individual, instead of labouring on appearances to produce them.

Thus a village, a house or even a bedside table, can become a contextual condition for solidarity, a platform analogously, practically and metaphorically. Within the boundary condition the context may be consolidated and incorporation made obtuse. On the other hand outside the boundary condition may be chaotic, dysfunctional, for a while or all the time according to the processing and the relationships between what have become phenomena with characteristics understood by all those on the platform and by others not on the platform but who process their appearances through what have emerged as not dissimilar passages and corridors. Since individual processing is potentially unhelpful for any homogenous, synchronous activities, we use the process of incorporation to direct what have become phenomena towards fixed or variable interactions without loss of functionality thus incorporation extends concepts of space and time, the media we make most use of on platforms, whilst seeking to retain belief/trust in relationships so that the illusion is maintained. We may believe the benefits will be an enhanced quality of experience in some way and that losses will be acceptable, whatever they are will never be experienced unless the processing for now is altered, of course. This raises issues about adaptation since the assumption of function is always modelled but linked to the benefits of "finding out", exploring or to knowing, confirming, re-establishing and so on. We will call these political economic issues indicating that in order to cope with experience, what is in fact contingent, we must find out more about new and radical appearances that appear in the now, sui-generis as indications of fecund possibility that may however bring about the obsolescence of existing solidarities and the suspension or dissolution of many platforms and thus many contexts or else we must absolutely attempt to avoid new and radical appearances which as we have said is impossible to achieve yet possible to articulate using our various media such as this one, writing, thus dictionaries.

The ticking clock and before it the calendar that used earth days and years reckoned by the disappearances of a sun and the arrivals of a moon, the henges for example, become relative to us in various ways because they confirm value relationships by their appearances and allow us to produce socialisations as correlative incorporations producing functionality that would be difficult to imagine without the use of phenomena that appear to us as measurements of time and space as we see in Fordism[31] replacing the more ambiguous relationships of pure imposition and aggression for example, force of arms or claims of superiority linked to spiritual forces and chance events such as lightning, duels and so on. We have elected to be related to the clock and to appearances in common incorporated correlatively, but the danger is that by using the clock and the built environment to determine the very experiences of life we avoid and ignore appearances that are unhelpful far too readily. Thus we remove processing from those very appearances that are unknown to us taking them as appearances to be ignored, not valued, rather than acknowledging that value is unavoidable and thus assimilation is also unavoidable making suppression and repression of any subsequent processing the only possible incorporation that can be allowed by one or by many if the incorporation is socialised. The potential values of removed appearances, those that never appear because we deny ourselves the opportunity must be held at a distance even though we now have convincing evidence, even in these pages, that many appearances will invade our processing and unsettle what must now be conceptualised on the transcendental platform of phenomena that are considered allowable, as the narcissistic elegance of what we believe is functional whereas we remain in the now of experience and humanity is no more a thing than it is nothing, it is process. Those appearances that bring function are brought closer to us as a working functionality and thus a practiced daily, weekly, monthly process. The true nature of our existence is the continuous processing of

---

[31] Time and motion studies in human productive systems

experience. Exploration is a necessity for functionality of any sort whilst practice is paradoxically practically functional yet removed from the real by every attempt to increase the functionality that we process it as being, rather than the one we experience which it really is albeit impossible to accommodate as a whole or exactly.

Chapter Six
Freedom

Exploring Pragmatism

Having at one time thought of my work as existentialist, even to the extent of putting on the cover of the work, and online, it now seems that is the wrong concept. Existention presumably implies an existence whereas what this work has developed is an approach to experiencing. This is different from experience, which I have consolidated into both a process of Incorporation and a resource which I call the construct. Solidarity appears as the effect of converting what was once <u>free</u> wiring into <u>fixed</u> wiring through a process of incorporation as a skill that articulates appearances as they appear as phenomena allowing functionality to emerge out of what otherwise are a series of contingent relationships between appearances. What exists cannot be accommodated other than as appearances that must be processed in order to produce functional relationships which occur because articulation is possible and epicentric phenomena interact relative to each other within part pattern relationships that can become rational by way of contextual boundaries that appear to us as phenomena and sets of phenomena involving both time and space as the result of processing and articulatory skills. These multi-layered part pattern and eventually bounded and thus part/whole contextual relationships transcend appearances to become models and/or narratives, articulations I have called them, using categories of time and space having analogue and metric values meaning that they are ambiguous until fixed. The fixing created by incorporation and solidarity as explained in the preceding chapters becomes as if utterly fixed with a propensity to require totalising and exact fixing which I claim is not possible except as metrics that cannot possibly relate totally to experience but give the distinct impression of existing or being. As a skill these models become reflexively incorporated and thus epicentric phenomena appear as me and I and we and so on as well as apples onions and crocodile tears.

We bring ourselves into an ambiguous existence and an ambiguous existence with phenomena all of which are experienced as existing in some way that must be explained using space and time together as a model of reality, we believe, that transcends its ambiguity. Extremes of ambiguity and tolerance attend the production of all models. We cope by assimilating appearances, producing phenomena, on the basis that appearances relate to phenomena which have to be produced in order to become reality allowing our articulations to produce a model as a process. We process appearances by accommodating them which is never exact, assimilating them along with aleatory and subliminal appearances and with synergy harvesting what emerges from the construct contemporaneously with the emergence of everything that emerges. In order to control accommodation there must be process, an articulation of appearances, incorporation, that is the gradually emerging reflexive processing producing phenomena that allows for functionality with univalent and intolerant processing resulting from conditioning, making the nervous system contain more and more reflexive corridors and processions.

We emerge out of this process as a body having several attributes which are having a brain or mind, being a person, having feelings and being capable of rationality. The way this body does things appears to be conditioned when we do things in the same way day after day after day as what is fixed becomes surrounded by more of what is fixed in an inevitable complex of related phenomena that "belong" in the spectacle having become a context for us. Some of those who study and ask questions about such issues [there are many more of the first than of the latter sort] use terms like embodied and embedded indicating the belief that there is a causal chain binding body to surroundings which we have explained is the effect of wiring becoming predisposed to alter appearances and making do with appearances that become phenomena relating functionally. A good analogous example is the sun rising, which we know it does not, but it appears to rise and therefore it becomes an appearance that is linked to a phenomenological relationship that is quite profoundly incorrect and yet part of the everyday performance of life for most people on the planet understood as a sun rising since relatively that is what we experience.

We appear to articulate sequential actions and/or scripted action just like a riff, as in jazz, a riff of spontaneous action repeated just as the cricket player bowls or the tennis player reacts to a service or a volley, or as a friend throws a bottle of water for us to catch impromptu and yet in the fairly certain belief that it is not aimed at our heads and intended as a friendly gesture on a hot day, or is indeed an attack and therefore a more pressing question and in each case we play the trump or ask the question; you **are** a friend or **are** you a friend? Are we a group or enemies, not friends?

Thus we evolve/develop in the very short term as children and strangers then perhaps for the rest of our lives we become hard wired and measured and what we allow and become reflexive, robotic, immune to appearances that do not matter in our own transcendental phenomenological model, licensed as we may call it. What is licensed is the platform on which we stand more or less firmly because of good deep processing or recently acquired processing that has yet to stand the effect of experience and our ineluctable processing of it. We belong to sui-generis and are bound by the processing that we experience. We are able to articulate what emerge as phenomena of time and space, particularly the body and its hands and brain, and create models that categorise some phenomena as belonging to the body and other to surroundings. We use these abilities, incorporation, to vote for a status quo that is the increasing reflexivity of the nervous system and its processing bringing about solidarity which is the fixing of contextual relationships so that deductive functional interactions appear to take place as real, experienced contemporaneously even though, as we have seen, they cannot do so. We also assume or believe in a past and future that is real even though, and even more so, this is not possible other than as a transcendental model using phenomena produced by us as a process sometimes entirely dependent upon contingency and the construct. Thus on the very first occasion of our question, as it is in the real, belief and proof are not necessarily linked by truth or by practice but by possibility alone, contingent in fact, prescient in evolutionary terms, as if waiting to happen, and thereafter, because of the bodies propensity to perform synergy directing any appearances that simultaneous necessity has thrown at us, we drink the water in the thrown bottle as an answer: you are a friend. The experience contributes towards the practice, The body we have and its labour power, potential processing, and the asset of experience is linked to the transcendental phenomena that themselves contribute to the process and tend to confirm or deny its efficacy, its efficiency in terms of articulation, incorporation, solidarity and capacity for socialisation as others synchronize their own processing with those with whom functionality achieves outcomes that are valued more or less.

The two diagrams that follow illustrate the way socialisation sits within the processing so that incorporation continues using the same relationships with the influences of socialisation adding to the reflexivity of incorporation. Diagram 6.1 shows the relationship between symbiosis, synergy and solidarity where processing represents each to the other in myriad connections through many epicentres with a propensity to reinforce links between neurons. Alterations to one will alter the other as propensities towards or away from solidarity. Diagram 6.2 shows how socialisation simply sits into the processing by altering solidarity and thus synergy via symbiosis.

Diagram 6.1 the emergence of solidarity

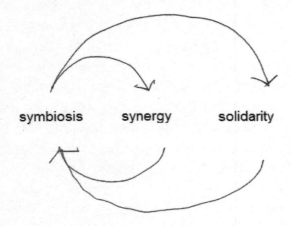

symbiosis   synergy   solidarity

Diagram 6.2 socialisation added

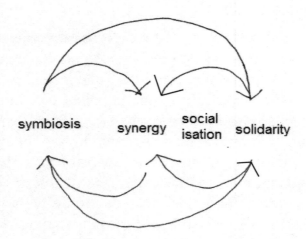

symbiosis   synergy   social   solidarity
                          isation

We are not yet used to dealing with experience as the issue. We are still in the process of articulating what we call an understanding of the transcendental phenomenological model as if it is real and historic and functional when correct because we have been convinced to believe that our processing would not be possible unless some efficient correlation presented itself to us. The belief is that it would not be right fair and proper if a correlation turned out to be chaotic and inefficient, as if our lives were meaningless and impossibly difficult. Of course our lives are possible and have meaning because of the processing done that appears to us as if we are doing it as interpreters of phenomenological appearances rather than as processors of appearances that we convert into phenomena and then articulate them in concert with their emergence from sui-generis so as to provide a model using time and space as categories of potential order.

We forget or never realise, are never taught, that we are socialised from birth. All the stories of individual babies brought up in the wild have been found to be untrue or wildly exaggerated. In the main we process as we have been conditioned so that the basic highways and byways of neural connectivity become reflexive fairly early on[32], actually they <u>must</u> be put in place since the neural system works on the basis of laying pathways for what works and ignoring what doesn't; incorporation is a two way street so to speak. Neural corridors and pathways become motorways and railway lines quite rapidly through a process called myelination that enhances speed so that one corridor will allow faster travel than others. All of this is a vulgar representation, admittedly, but it enhances and reinforces the proposition that experience is a process in which we produce the phenomena that we

---

[32] Blakemore S J, Frith U

believe ourselves to be. We produce all phenomena and many of them most in fact, will be the products of socialisation that have been around for millennia before now. Varieties of socialisation will alter the propensity to use phenomena of one sort or another and the media and categories of those that some social groups have whilst others do not[33]. What appear to be phenomena because of the excellent articulation we have as part of processing deludes or flatters us into believing that we act upon the phenomena rather than the appearances which is of course the effect of functional interaction. It is of course seemingly what happens and gives rise to the belief that phenomena exist. This then gives rise to the question of existence and we have the paradox of rhetorical confrontation using the very phenomena created by what we are struggling to explore. The very reflexive properties of the conditioned correlative interactions prevent us from exploring the appearances themselves unless we are for example mad, scientists or artists, struggling to get behind each phenomenon to find what it really is, only to find there is nothing except emergence, the process of producing the phenomena and our interactions with them; hence back to the process as the complexity turned into simple function, our propensity towards the metric forgetting it is a transcending of contingency.

The major exposure of process is as Winnecott's contribution, amongst others, when something that should not have happened happens and something that should have happened does not happen[34]. If we transpose the should not and should to the concept of contradiction and paradox we find that

---

[33] Brown D E
[34] Winnecott D W

experience of these alert our processing to the possibility that not only excellence in functionality may potentially exist, the ideal and the utopian, but also the cataclysmic and dystopian, the awful and the impossible to bear may also exist and so anxiety about both perfection and dread are transcendental possibilities.

Dealing with experience as if it is stable and fixed, that we simply have to explore it to find functional options, is a problematic option taken up by many forcing them to invent chance and good and bad luck to account for what cannot otherwise be explored since the phenomenological model can only include metaphysics as an answer, symbolic references that cover up for what actually happens. Unfortunately the obvious alternative, dealing only with the processing and paying close attention to it is not an available option since the processing already does that. In the latter case however processing with an understanding of the process allows us to use processing to process what might lay behind the metaphysical edge and even create phenomena to model underlying parts of the process. We have experience of doing this during the last century and more. We did it with various media, drawing and maths, those media that lend themselves to both processing and the production of phenomena that can be socialised, appear to others as similar appearances at least.

The propensity for pragmatism which has overtaken our lives in the west linking us to what we often call rationalism and mental ability [sic] seems to require the subjugation of what we call emotions which are the analogue values also known as opinions and to some degree freedom. Rationalism and instrumentalism, the reflexive processing of functional interactions with phenomena leading to anxieties about perfection and failure or lack of function become a reality because our processing transcends experience replacing it with a model of reality so convincing we worry that it may never be perfect, not really be true. Both fears are correct and yet overstated but pragmatism operates as a repressive factor on these fears whilst at the same time promoting them. The worst processing of all considers the pragmatic to be the only possible answer and suppresses all other possibilities. This leads to paradoxical and contradictory outcomes eventually as we see from processes in political economies around the globe none of which have progressed from existential questions to those which explore the process and modify its parts. Typically for example in the UK the democratic process, quite advanced politically and economically in global terms of processing the voices of all citizens, still makes parliamentary decisions that are pragmatic because fixed as legal texts. Rather than ask what we are producing its citizens demand to know what to do, and how to do it, who they are and what will become of them? These are questions asked by things not by processes.

It will be difficult but not impossible in my opinion to start producing the phenomenon of an I that asks what experiences are currently processed and what epicentric phenomena relate to it and on what basis the relationships should or could be contained with a context or contexts such that they become ambiguous or exact according to the processing applied to the appearances in question as to the content, form and context in which appearances take up their phenomenological transcendence. As a teacher I know that my experience of architectural education was about just such an appreciation of processing. My students were entirely happy about knowing it, and we were careful to understand that tiredness, hunger and thermal extremes, particularly of cold, were dangerous conditions in which to process any appearances at all except those encountered during sleep. This is not to say that the struggle of exploration is easy, it is not and is often challenging but design, architectural design, is not just about built phenomena but about the matter of solidarity itself and of course socialisation.

When going around an art gallery or a science museum we see the products of exploration of the sort I am processing now. These are products of hand and brain, together in both cases, art and science and design is merely the integration of this explorative processing with reflexive pragmatic processing so that each explores the other, which is the subject of this chapter "freedom" that needs the subject of the next when socialised.

Chapter Seven

D.E.P.T.H

The essential processing of individuals on their own is labouring that converts into working as functioning by incorporation becoming a solidarity with a context as a functional result or not becoming functional. What is functional is not what we call normal but reflexive to processing however it becomes normal for any solidarity in which the specific solidarity works, functions. The correlation between our processing and processing in general is of course that of time and space that lasts and correlates to our reflexive behaviours. Our wonderfully adaptive and improvisational abilities that we are born with, notwithstanding the fact that our nervous system rapidly develops corridors and passageways that in effect begin to control genotypical processing we remain capable of laying down alternative pathways. In addition the original laying of pathways is not always that certain. Thus we have, as we know from experience, those who are able to change their reflexive behaviours and those that have reflexive behaviours rather more unique than others. In addition we have those who slavishly follow whatever behaviours have been established in that original laying out of the pathways of the nervous system. These routes through the nervous system are being investigated now building on the work done over the last two hundred years and more, meaning that hypotheses, conjectures, guessing, has taken place and will continue to take place so long as we live. Individual freedom is for me the freedom to challenge the original laying out of routes and adding some adaptive routing as best I can. Often the original routes work, mainly because it seems that this correlation with what is processed in time and space other than the genotype provides us with a human environment at least in terms of what is processed. Thus plants have cycles and years in which they alter, buildings have cycles in which they alter very little once built, but do not exist at all unless we produce them. Once built buildings last for as long as the weather and contingency do not decay and demolish them.

I have laid down what I believe about the processing and so far as I have done so I believe it correlates to what is currently understood, albeit written up in a vulgar manner, which is to say neuroscientists will argue as they must over detail but the general scheme of processing is that we produce phenomena out of appearances all of which emerge out of sui-generis such that everything emerges out of nothing and we process along with all processing such that we must cope with everything or be dysfunctional. Coping does not mean processing everything nor does it mean articulating, the word I use for incorporating the propensities that the original laying out of roads and the gradual adaptive and improvisational laying out of roads brings with incorporation. Once the old and new roads are laid solidarity follows as night follows day, the circadian rhythms and dialectical homeostasis ensure that as much as the genotype allows with phenotypical variations. The asset of each phenotype, which is the construct, the mass accumulation of experience of the process, is a constant dialectic between experience and sui-generis, the emergence of everything and nothing, that we are part of, we do not process what emerges but are the process of emergence that we are contained within as our real condition.

What we notice about experience then is this difference in movement and completion between foxes and foxgloves and furniture, for example. The differences are obvious to us and emerge from their own processing within emergence[35]. The routes through our nervous system correlate with these other processes in the sense that they take account of the properties that emerge, such is the nature of the nervous system that it is a reflexive organ that has no choice other than to do so. Thus whereas an artist can articulate the possibility of a plant that walks, and articulate phenomena so as to express that as plausible, plants cannot do so. What humanity does now, whatever it did four million years ago when it stood on its own two feet, is this articulation of phenomena by hand and brain in addition to the processing of appearances. I have tried to show how phenomena themselves are obviously subjected again and again to emergence as a process and that this confirms the qualitative properties of appearances, especially when they actually are related to phenomena such that they too appear again and again making it possible for the nervous system to lay down motorways in place of simple foot prints across a virgin field.

The way both Kant and Hegel more recently made their contributions was to express this human environment as the transcendental environment. They did not exactly contribute that but that is the contribution I take from them. This transcendental environment is not full of things but full of

---

[35] Holland J H

phenomena that appear to us. Along with these phenomena are appearances that appear out of sui-generis along with everything that appears to us. These appearances are processed according to our location relative to them all, usually on earth, during a day or night time period, often hemmed in by appearances of a substantial processing strength such as buildings, forests, savannah and so on, and often trammelled by the actions of others, getting on or off buses, trains, horses and bicycles. This processing constantly lays down tracks, lanes, roads, streets, motorways and in addition we can fly in neurological terms when the maybe of the synaptic cleft [see diagram 2.4 page 35], the dendritic connection, is used to call all cells within range of chemical encouragement to contribute to a processing need[36].

Such freedom that exists is the freedom to explore what is otherwise reflexively produced and it is the production of it that our processing does as an emergent processing over which we have this very limited control to appeal by way of any impasse or contradiction or paradox that appears to us mainly of course because the sweet and functional experience is altered and appears to us as chaotic, a word we can use in English to refer to such paradoxical conditions in experience. As I will show in the second and third volumes of this trilogy we can, and some will, inevitably, articulate millions of words, like this, over even the use of chaotic as a term that adequately defines the experience I am trying to illustrate, show, conjecture. This is where we have got to now, an ability to articulate phenomena all of which emerge out of a process

---

[36] Greenfield S

over which we have limited if any control, the latter, if any, particularly if we do not seek to be free, as we say, if we do, and thus are happy with what we refer to as the status quo. In the other two volumes the conditional sense will be dropped a little since, as with the sun is rising as an example, it becomes tedious once the concept of the fact of referral to a colloquialism is acknowledged by anyone having a conversation with another, which is what I hope this is, a conversation rather than a polemic, as much as I can manage with a book at least.

Our articulation of phenomena means that at the very least we commonly rather than individually deal with transcendental phenomena, those which have been produced and are known by their effects on that processing. We often call this their effects upon us, but that is not the case since the us are individuals each of whom, as this book explains in previous chapters, re read them if this is still not clear to you, process individually using a genotype that ensures that at least some of the neural pathways are laid to a common pattern, but not all and none of those after the age of twenty four years or so. That is when the body ceases its developmental growth from birth and starts its developmental growth of maturity, like a tree, early growth, mature growth, maturity, death. Early growth is mostly if not always socialised. Mature growth is almost always socialised. Maturity is often varied between all sorts of socialisation. All of these socialisations actually occur as more or less, on their way to or at, reflexive solidarities so that I have even used the term platform to indicate the nature of the solidarity as a platform under which the neural pathways provide a structure upon which the incorporator stands. This is the transcendental phenomenological platform that processes everything that has become solid into phenomena out of appearances that emerge out of sui-generis and are rapidly, because reflexive, thus automatically so to speak, processed into phenomena that may then be articulated into the ongoing articulation that we experience as action by hand and brain.

This platform and these platforms that join together to form a socialisation like scales on a fish or pebbles on a beach are all produced out of nothing, sui-generis, emerging first as appearances then because processing is not a sequence but a contemporaneous experience, as phenomena, having the qualities of correlation with solidarities, incorporations and thus common or socialised functionalities, not necessarily one but many since these platforms are not made of stone but cannot return to sui-generis because they never leave it, sui-generis is ever present, the appearances and the phenomena rely upon recursive experiences of themselves and through processing so that the laying of routes, corridors and roadways can take place.

The adaptive and improvisational characteristic of the individual is thus not simple or immediate other than as propensities established by rules of emergence. A building cannot simply appear overnight unless it is a very complex technical engineering feat that we have now learnt to produce. Up until one hundred years ago such feats were only imagined and buildings often took over one hundred years to produce, cathedrals for example, were started, fell down, continued, shifted and then rebuilt[37]. These experiences, including the

---

[37] Addis B

now built and repeat appearance of cathedrals, are processed and accumulated as assets in the construct, the term I use for this continuous harvesting of experience that is maintained as the status quo of the nervous system in sui-generis which it never leaves. This characteristic of sui-generis is the nothingness out of which all appearances emerge. What we consider to be past and future, but particularly for us the past, is what we produce by articulating phenomena that have been produced by our processing. In order to understand what is on any platform we have to consider the following points.

Firstly what is on the platform may or may not be articulated with any skill whatsoever and indeed the phenomena may be articulated in specifically individual ways as well as ways that have become socialised by early growth, mature growth or death for example, particularly the death of the status-quo which can occur in anyone at any time. This death of the status-quo is the solidarity fixed resolutely by routine and work in what I call the obtuse mode of production. In all five modes of production emerge out of individual processing and these are shown in diagram 7.1.

Diagram 7.1 the categories of processing that appear to us

I.   Chaotic

II. Abductive

III. Inductive

IV. Deductive

V.   Obtuse

I suggest that as we use our skills of articulation to move around and to think, wag the tongue and write, all of which articulate phenomena in order to indicate part pattern and perhaps part whole if we can, that means we attempt to shift from category I to category V, so that we thereby refer to specific deductive relationships between phenomena that have, remember, been produced from individual processing and thus are unique to individuals and yet socialised in their categorical relationships. What this means is that for some the obtuse will appear chaotic, although in the main it means that any obtuse will appear at least inductive and then deductive and then, gradually or especially confrontationally, obtuse.

In terms of the human condition what I have described is our propensity to produce phenomena out of appearances that emerge out of sui-generis such that the process allows phenomena to emerge onto a transcendental platform which has the properties of appearing along with other appearances and transcending them, hence transcendental, because we have or are in the process of laying down neural pathways or corridors for the reflexive production of phenomena that emerge as mattering to us because they become assets that we accumulate by way of propensities to act upon them by hand and brain so that they allow us to function.

These phenomena emerge out of the dialectical process I have described in earlier chapters and it is a process unique to each individual and yet has a propensity to emerge as a genotype with phenotypical properties as described, above. Thus each and every platform is unique in its specificities whilst sharing the genotypical propensity to process appearances. The tricky part of interpreting the relationships between individual processing and genotypical processing has a reference which is hermeneutics[38]. This introduces a term which is, as with chaos, highly contested and so will be dealt with in volume two of this trilogy. In brief however it is the interpretive effort required to sort out the propensities within the individual processing as well as the articulation of phenomena so that some sort of overall assessment may be made as to the context and the relationships between phenomena within any solidarity and, to greater or lesser extents, within any emerging solidarity that is being incorporated contemporaneously. The title of this chapter DEPTH is my acronym for dialectical existential phenomenological transcendental hermeneutics. The dialectical part is the processing itself, the existential part is the belief required by any transcendental articulation that phenomena have relationships to other phenomena and what values they have in both analogue and metric values. The existential argument over what exists on the platform is just that, what exists on the platform and not what exists, which is probably the most important part of this version of existentialism. It is not arguing over soul or spirit or metaphysics of any sort at all but over processing and its possibilities. As we interpret phenomena, the products of processing by individuals, we must note the creativity of that production. As individuals show a propensity to move towards analogue values they lose the capacity to articulate phenomena and allow phenomena to in effect articulate

---

[38] Bleicher J

themselves as it were through processing alone[39]. As individuals more towards the opposite of introspection which is say, extrospection, exploration amongst metric values they delimit the accuracy of what previously appeared to them as exactly functional relevant to their processing of values such as good and bad, functional and chaotic. These moves are essential creative tools and the main purpose of this book is to open up debate to all individuals interested in creativity.

Diagram 7.2 The understanding in DEPTH

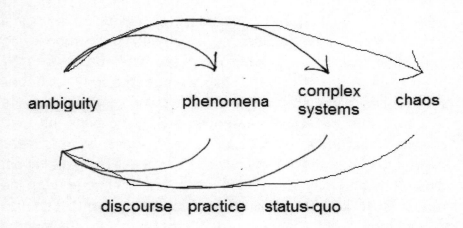

We used these moves in our studio work in the architectural department in the University of Ulster when I was in charge of all the cultural context modules there. Unfortunately once I

---

[39] We have become used to call this emotional behaviour but I am hoping to challenge this description and rename it aware or awake, at least.

retired my courses were dumped because I had not brought them to a point where they could be taught by others, not a good situation for a teacher to be in! So I have worked on my own and gradually articulated this book, Smile, with subsequent volumes currently outlined, part complete, to form a trilogy, and feel that the work is at last able to be carried on by other teachers all of whom must be for ever students and thus to be carried on by all students of creativity. It will also help those who attempt to maintain a status-quo by offering them a therapeutic understanding of paradox and contradiction in any obtuse condition.

DEPTH, dialectical existential phenomenological transcendental hermeneutics, is a contribution to processing that once included will have its effect upon processing by making us aware at the articulatory stage, the transcendental phenomenological stage, that we are articulating phenomena that are, immediately, appearences processed back into part of any individuals processing should those appearances appear to that or those individuals. Thus books have an impact when read and may, quite often, effect a total change upon the reader, such as Abbe Raynal's work on imperialism[40] that was earlier than Saint Simon's and seems to have effected the processing of slaves such that the Haitian Revolution emerged out of the status quo that was the slave trade of England, France and Spain at that time, 216 years before now.

We can achieve this hermeneutic using the basic yes, no maybe that is all the processing of the nervous system is capable of apart from throwing the maybe open to all who can

[40] Raynal A

respond to it. The epicentric phenomena, all of them, remain individually processed so that what we find with functional behaviour is not normal but individual functional behaviour. and the only way to correlate it to the behaviour of all of us is to apply the hermeneutic approach which is not to discover the author but the epicentricity of any functional behaviour, a sort of star gazing at the individuals model of phenomenological transcendence which must be assembled as phenomena with ambivalence until we establish analogue and metric values that allow discourse and practice and eventually solidarity to emerge. This is the sort of thing that Rorty[41] and Habermas[42] suggest we do which is to engage in conversation, with the reader, their followers and so on, rather than agonistic rhetoric, which is what an awful lot of socialists and politicians in general have learnt to do because they are hoping to win rather than deal with process. Coming back to dear Zizek for a moment this rhetorical approach is his metier which he articulates with great skill and charm to those who are not his enemies. I would certainly not welcome becoming his enemy nor do I need to worry, I believe, since if ever I do come to his attention, appear to him, or my work to him, he would recognise the contributions his work has made to mine and I recognise them as his championing not the rhetoric, which has become a necessary part of the epicentric phenomenological battle of academe and publishing and so on, professors and their positions, but his familiarity with the problems of nothingness that are shared by too few writers and academics and philosophers now.   The practice of philosophers have

---

[41] Rorty R
[42] Habermas J

potential effects by way of appearances even over millennia, see texts and buildings as examples, each of which can be used as appearances in processing at any time so long as they still appear to us[43] and influence our processing individually if we are free to allow the propensities of their influences.

In political economic terms the processing that individuals do is their only source of freedom since even if socialisation offers it the individual must take up that offer and then can only process within the milieu of social practices in general as they appear all around; it will be a struggle as many students of creative endeavours, especially in my own experience, architects, find to their dismay. Appearances emerging from sui-generis do so and quickly become processed reflexively or not according to the propensity of each individual to incorporate using reflexive or non reflexive pathways that have developed or are developing with the nervous system. It is a process of experiencing that is never experienced, there is no looking back, only the processing that produces phenomena that we have this ability to articulate, it is articulation that we humans manage and that is a skill acquired by practice in exactly, almost, the same way as we practice serving at tennis or eating with chopsticks.

The non-reflexive is not functional within a solidarity but then the reflexive is never going to be perfect. The most we can claim is that socialisation using reflexive processing will be at best pragmatic and less than perfect given adequate conditioning and popularity and that without conditioning and

---

[43] For example poems and plays and songs may appear even from centuries, it is talk, discourse, that appears briefly yet has influence

the use of non-reflexive conditioning chaos has a propensity to emerge out of processing rather than synchronic functionality[44].

The best we can manage given the impossibility of producing phenomena out of thin air other than by processing appearances as they are experienced, processed, contemporaneously harvesting experience massed as an asset in the nervous system as a whole in sui-generis, encouraging propensities via the dialectical interaction between symbiosis and synergy in some way, to explore using epicentric phenomena, articulation and making contextual boundaries become thin and non-existent, so as to deliberately challenge what may otherwise become too reflexive. I have categorised these as steps moving from chaos, through abductive and inductive to deductive and finally obtuse solidarity using this process described as incorporation. When we incorporate it becomes functional and then a solidarity for individuals on a platform that requires depth of understanding as in DEPTH. As experience shifts from feeling inept, out of control, lost to that of understanding, which is the term for articulating functionally in one of the five categories [beyond which we have presumably drugged, drunk, asleep and comatose conditions of experience. Politically the freedom of individuals is not subject to any other individual without this dialectical understanding that emerges from processing that must commence with labouring, turning it into work, functional

---

[44] Note that herding, copying strangers, appears to us as a phenomenon but this seems to relate to processing units that have been located in the nervous system and produce empathetic copying, so work in progress on this then but generally categorised as subliminal perhaps?

interactions with phenomena produced by the processes of incorporation, solidarity and socialisation. Understanding is not of the transcendental phenomenological model but our efforts at incorporation that include introspection and extrospection together with the dialectical processing that is experiencing constantly processing what emerges as appearances from sui-generis. These appearances are constantly and relentlessly processed into phenomena that must be acted upon as necessitated by their relationships to each other hence the contextual relationship to phenomena that are themselves contextually related to appearances that have created values that are analogue and metric measures allowing functionality to emerge such that values are placed appropriately for the necessities of continuing with our experiencing.

This book is for teachers who will remain students so that they learn from those they teach. I believe it will be especially helpful to artists and scientists, those at the cutting edge of articulatory practices, as well as any others who remain students of life rather than obtuse experts in a field. We must find a way to work together creatively!

Books That Help
To Make Us Smile *and a postscript*

In no particular order

Brunswick E, 1947/1956, Perception and the Representative Design of Psychological Experiments, Berkeley California, University of California Press

Kolakowsky L, Main Currents of Marxism, W W Norton + Co., New York, London, 1976, translated by Falla P S, 1978, 2005 paperback version used

Zizek S, Mao on Practice and Contradiction, Verso, London and New York, 2007

Krauss L M, A Universe from Nothing, Simon & Shuster, UK, 2012

Laing R D, The Divided Self, Harmondsworth, Penguin Books, 1975

Churchland P M, The Engine of Reason the Seat of the Soul, MIT, 1995

Donald M, Origins of the Modern Mind, London; Cambridge Ma, Harvard Uni Press, 1991

Fodor J, The Language of Thought, Hassocks, Harvester Press, 1976

Fodor J, The Mind Doesn't Work That Way, MIT Press, 2000

Ryle G, The Concept of Mind, Penguin, 1990

Ott C J, The Evolution of Perception and the Cosmology of Substance, I Universe inc, Lincoln, 2004

Chomsky N, Syntactic Structures, Mouton, The Hague, 1957

Bickerton D, Language and Human Behaviour, University College Press, 1996

Durkheim E, Pragmatism and Sociology, Cambridge UK New York USA, Cambridge University Press, 1983, translation by Whitehouse J C

Plato, Theaitetos (part), London, J M Dent & sons, Tr.Warrington J, 1961

McGilchrist I, The Master and His Emissary, Yale University Press, New Haven and London, 2010

Mlodinow. L, Subliminal, Random House USA Inc, New York/US, 2012

Rorty R, Philosophy and the Mirror of Nature, Oxford, Blackwell, 1980

Schrag C O, The Resources of Rationality, Indiana, Indiana University Press, 1992

Schrag C O, Communicative Praxis and the Space of Subjectivity, Indiana, Indiana Press, 1986

De Saussure F, (1915), Course in General Linguistics, Duckworth, 1983

Dewey J Bentley A F, Knowing and the Known, 1949, Beacon Press

Hayek F A, The Sensory Order, The University of Chicago Press, Chicago Illinois, 1976

Peirce C S, 1931, Elements of Logic – Collected Papers Vol II, Belnap Press, Massachusetts, 1960

Edelman G, Bright Air, Brilliant Fire, Penguin, 1994

Csapo E, Theories of Mythology, Blackwell, Oxford, 2005

Swift J, Gulliver's Travels, 1735,

Damasio A R, Descartes Error, Picador, 1995

Leader D, What is Madness? Hamish Hamilton, Penguin Books, 2011

Sherrington C S, (1906), The Integrative Action of the Nervous System, New York, Arno Press, 1973

Searle J R, The Construction of Social Reality, Allen Lane, 1995

Wilson E O, Consilience, London, Little Brown, 1998

Lyotard J F, The Post Modern Condition, Manchester, Manchester University Press, 1994

Malraux A, Museum without Walls, Garden City New York, Doubleday, 1967, tr. Gilbert S Price F

Dietrich A, The Cognitive Neuroscience of Creativity, Psychonomic Bulletin and Review, 2004, 11 (6), pp.1011-1026

Jones S, The Language of the Genes, London, Harper Collins, 1993

Voegelin E, Science Politics & Gnosticism, ISI Books, Wilmington Delaware, 2004

Arendt H, The Human Condition, Chicago, University of Chicago Press, 1969 [to page 174]

Harman G, The Quadruple Object, Zero Books, Hants UK, 2011

McLuhan M, Understanding Media, London, Routledge+Keegan Paul, 1964

Greenfield S, The Human Brain, Phoenix, 2000

Rose S, The 21st Century Brain, London, Jonathan Cape, 2005

Holland J H, Emergence From Chaos to Order, Helix Books Addison Wesley, 1998

Reason J, Human Error, Cambridge, Cambridge University Press, 1992

Brown D E, Human Universals, New York, McGraw Hill, 1991

Simmel G, the Philosophy of Money, London and New York, Routledge, 2004

LeDoux J, 1996, The Emotional Brain, New York, Simon and Schuster

Zizek S, Less Than Nothing, Verso, London and New York, 2013

Zizek S, The Sublime Object of Ideology, Verso, London and New York, 1989

Addis B, Building, Phaidon Press, 2007

Prigogene I, Is Future Given? Singapore, world Scientific Publishing, 2003

Lacan J, Ecrits A Selection, London, Tavistock, 1977

Geertz C, 1973, The Interpretation of Cultures, London, Fontana Press, 1993

Vattimo G, 1985/1988, The End of Modernity, Cambridge, Polity Press

Einstein A, The Theory of Relativity, Methuen + Co., 1920

Mitchell M, Complexity a Guided Tour, Oxford University Press, New York New York, 2011

Engels F, The Housing Question, The Cooperative Publishing Society of Foreign Workers in the USSR, Moscow and Leningrad, 1935

Machiavelli N, The Prince, Penguin, 1981

Yalom I D, Existential Psychotherapy, Basic, New York, 1980

Calvin W H, The River that Runs Uphill, The Sierra Club, 1986

Plotkin H, The Nature of Knowledge, Allen Lane, 1994

Vaneigem R, The Revolution of Everyday Life, London, Rebel Press/Left Bank Books, 1994, translated by Nicholson-smith D

Blakemore S J, Frith U, The Learning Brain, Oxford, Malden US, Carlton Oz, 2001

Winnecott D W, Human Nature, Free Association Books, 1988

Habermas J, Justification and Application, Polity Press, Cambridge, 1993

Bleicher J, The Hermeneutic Imagination, Routledge, London, 1982

Raynal A, A Philosophical and Political History of the Settlements and Trade of the Europeans in the East and West Indies, Negro Universities Press, New York, 1969

Badiou A, Logics of Worlds, Bloomsbury Academic, London-New York, 2009

The Postscript

The Architecture of Socialisation

I grew up in the forties loved and cared for by a couple who adopted me as their own son and laboured all their lives to produce a worthwhile member of society as they believed was necessary. Before he died my dad asked me where he went wrong and having thought about it I don't think he did go wrong, nor my mam. Both of them loved me even though I was the usual know it all kid with a lot to learn.

I went through architectural education like a knife through butter until I came up against the establishment. It threw me out of my stupor and made me realise that architecture as making buildings relied upon a status-quo that applied its values transcendentally and therefore erroneously.

And thus began the labours of bill the student, working on building sites, treading the boards in the fringe in Edinburgh and London, serving on tables and winning, and losing, at love and wine bars. Returning to architecture, and love, by way of environmental psychology and still labouring, contributing the cultural context modules to a brand new course of architecture in Belfast University of Ulster including an MSc course aiming to shift our understanding of architecture towards more than just something built. Whatever I thought that meant at the time, I was retired by jet lag at 65 leaving me to labour over this, the first of three volumes that sets out the basis on which we may proceed with an approach to understanding as a first step to changing the human condition.

The philosophies of humanism and capitalism must give way to a more civilised existence as it emerges from two thousand years of internecine arguments over the way we refer to our place in being, as Heidegger might have said.

We are beginning to understand enough about the human condition to realise that we can make and share functions heterogeneously. Even extremes are possible if we refrain from obtuse attitudes and acknowledge the political economic use of money as a way of linking individual values to social and public action at various scales of contextual relevance and phenomenological transcendence. Unfortunately for those of us alive at the moment, this will take a lot more work.

Just as individuals need time and space for periods of adjustment relating to the stresses inherent in transcendent beliefs so solidarities, corporations, institutions and myths wax and wane; Smile calls it understanding and this book is a small contribution offering itself as a primer for the task using DEPTH [chapter 7]. Exploration, dialogue and the possibility of mutual understanding through articulation and extrapolation are all elements in the revolution required so that internecine wars may become dialectical political economic conversations, attracting the support of those who would rather find a better use of their labouring than have it wedded to an erroneous extrapolation. As it turns out, architecture is a very good introduction to the human condition that we **must** learn to live with because otherwise we suffer unnecessarily.

Dr. Bill Thompson architect 2014